*Russell's
Metaphysical
Logic*

CSLI Lecture Notes
Number 101

Russell's Metaphysical Logic

Bernard Linsky

 CSLI Publications
*Center for the Study of
Language and Information
Stanford, California*

Copyright © 1999
CSLI Publications
Center for the Study of Language and Information
Leland Stanford Junior University
Printed in the United States
03 02 01 00 99   5 4 3 2 1

Library of Congress Cataloging-in-Publication Data

Linsky, Bernard.
Russell's metaphysical logic / Bernard Linsky.
p.   cm. — (CSLI lecture notes ; no. 101)
Includes bibliographical references.

ISBN 1-57586-209-3 (alk. paper).
ISBN 1-57586-210-7 (pbk. : alk. paper)

1. Russell, Bertrand, 1872–1970. 2. Logic. 3. Metaphysics.
I. Title. II. Series.
B1649.R94L56   1999
192—dc21   99-31299
CIP

∞ The acid-free paper used in this book meets the minimum requirements of
the American National Standard for Information Sciences—Permanence of
Paper for Printed Library Materials, ANSI Z39.48-1984.

CONTENTS

ACKNOWLEDGMENTS

Edward Zalta has worked through two different versions of this text providing extensive corrections and encouragement. I am also grateful to Darryl Jung and Chris Swoyer for comments. Gregory Landini and Allen Hazen provided extensive written remarks. Rachel Fitz provided helpful copy editing. I owe an enormous debt to my father, Leonard Linsky,who has taught me about Russell's logic over the years as though it were the family business, and who has generously encouraged me in writing a book that is different from the one he always intended to write. Finally, I would like to dedicate this book to my wife Elizabeth Millar, for all the patience and love she has shown while I worked at this thing.

Four of these chapters rely heavily on previously published papers. Chapter 2 is based on "Propositional Functions and Universals in *Principia Mathematica*", *Australasian Journal of Philosophy* 66, Dec., 447-460, (B. Linsky, [1988]) and portions are reprinted here with the permission of Oxford University Press. Chapter 3 derives from "Why Russell Abandoned Russellian Propositions" (B. Linsky, [1993]), in *Russell and Analytic Philosophy*, A.D. Irvine and G.A. Wedeking, eds., Toronto: University of Toronto Press, 193–209, and material is reprinted with the permission of the University of Toronto Press. Chapter 6 is based on "Was the Axiom of Reducibility a Principle of Logic?", (B. Linsky, [1990]) in *Early Analytic Philosophy: Frege, Russell, Wittgenstein*, W.W. Tait, ed., Chicago: Open Court, 1997, 107–121, and appears with the permission of Carus Publishing Company. Chapter 7 is based on "Russell's Logical Constructions" (B. Linsky, [1995]).

Russell's Changing Ontology

Bertrand Russell is notorious for having changed his philosophical views several times over the course of his career. In fact these frequent changes have made Russell somewhat unique among figures in the history of philosophy. A conflict between different texts by one philosopher is usually seen as a challenge to the scholar. One must either reconcile the two views or else pick one as "official" and rule the second to be a remnant of earlier views or an anticipation of later ones. This presumption has never held for Russell. Conflicts in his texts are almost always seen as a sign that his views changed rapidly, perhaps even in the course of writing one work. While very much a fresh approach in much of the history of philosophy, this view is a stale orthodoxy when it comes to Russell.[1] In this book I resist this tendency and attempt to reconcile Bertrand Russell's logical work, in particular the logic of *Principia Mathematica* [PM], with his various writings on metaphysics from the same period and later. My reconciliation will make sense of some of the problematic features of that logic, especially as they are defended in the introduction to the first edition of PM.[2] My account will also serve a broader pur-

---

[1] Paul Hager [1994] also resists this tendency, concentrating on Russell's epistemology, rather than his logic and metaphysics.

[2] PM was a great work of collaboration. It is certain that Russell was largely responsible for writing the introduction to PM and several of the logical notions such as that of descriptions and the no-class theory, are his work exclusively. As a result I will frequently speak of PM as though it were Russell's work, rather than saying that "Russell and Whitehead say that ...". When referring to the technical contents of PM, however, I will attribute the views to both, in order to stress that they come from PM rather than other works by Russell. Hylton [1990] presents four pieces of evidence for this common attribution of the foundational aspects of PM to Russell. First, there is Russell's own remark in "My Philosophical Development" ([MPD], 57), "Broadly speaking, Whitehead left the philosophical problems to me." Second, Whitehead's letter to the editor of *Mind* ([1926], 130), and third, his remarks in *Process and Reality* ([1929], 10n6), both saying that the material revised from the first edition, including the introduction had been originally Russell's. Finally, and primarily, there are the internal similiarities between PM and Russell's own "Mathematical Logic as

pose by revealing the close connection between logical and metaphysical investigations in Russell's mind, a connection that disappeared in the later development of analytic philosophy.

Beginning with "The Relation of Universals and Particulars" [RUP] in 1908 through *The Problems of Philosophy* [PoP] in 1912, the *Theory of Knowledge* [ToK] manuscript of 1913, and the *Philosophy of Logical Atomism* [PLA] in 1918, Russell engages in many discussions of ontology, especially on the nature of universals and particulars and the existence and nature of propositions and facts. Though his views change during this period a core of common views is easily found. Russell's views of logical ontology changed radically during the years after *Principles of Mathematics* [PoM] and only settled down with the actual writing of *Principia Mathematica*. By 1908 Russell had abandoned his long standing use of propositions as the basis of logic and also his various attempts to resolve the paradoxes without accepting a doctrine of types. He finally accepted propositional functions as logically fundamental, with a theory of types of functions as the basis for resolution of the paradoxes. His logical views then stayed constant until the second edition of *Principia* in 1925. Russell indicates no changes since PM in his logic in the *Introduction to Mathematical Philosophy* [IMP] of 1919 which is a synoptic, albeit popular, presentation of his logicist program. My attempts at a unified account of Russell will concentrate on this period from 1908 to 1919, arguing both that there is a unity in Russell's metaphysical views during this period and that the metaphysics is compatible with his logic, indeed it motivates or at least explains many of the features of that logic.

The large scale features of Russell's logical views are well known and not much disputed. Interpretive problems appear in technical aspects of the logic and, in what I will focus on, its connection with Russell's broader philosophy as expressed in the introduction to *Principia* and in his non-logical works. To help place the particular problems discussed below, here is a brief review of the main outlines of Russell's logic. Russell's first major logical project was his *Principles of Mathematics* from 1903, a statement and beginning of the *logicist* program of reducing mathematics to logic. This reduction consisted of defining mathematical notions in terms of logical notions, and then deriving mathematical principles by logical means alone. When almost finished with that book, Russell returned to a more careful study of Gottlob Frege's publications and in so doing discovered his famous paradox.[3] Previous discussions of

---

Based on the Theory of Types" [ML]. The details of the collaboration form a gap in our otherwise detailed knowledge of Russell's career.

[3]See G. Moore's introduction to *The Collected Papers of Bertrand Russell*, Vol. 3 [CP3] for details of the origin of the paradox.

classes, including Frege's, had assumed that for any predicate there is a class of things satisfying that predicate, its extension. Indeed, logicians considered classes to be simply the extensions of predicates, and hence distinctively logical entities. Russell's paradox arises directly out of this assumption. Classes may be members of other classes. It should make sense to at least say that a class is, or is not, a member of itself. Consider the predicate 'is a class that does not belong to itself'. This predicate will have an extension, the class of all those classes that are not members of themselves. Russell then asks: is that class a member of itself? If it is, then it falls within the extension of the predicate "is not a member of itself" and so it is not a member of itself. If it is not a member of itself, by similar reasoning, it appears that it is a member of itself. This is the contradiction. This paradox is described in the finished version of PoM along with several others. Another, which Russell included with the paradox of classes in his famous letter to Frege, does not involve classes, but is instead directly stated in terms of predicates. Russell ([PoM], 80) asks us to consider the notion of a predicate applying to itself. While most predicates will not be predicable of themselves, some will. Thus 'non-humanity' is not human, and so is self predicable. Consider then the predicates which are not predicable of themselves. They are those that satisfy the predicate 'is not predicable of itself'. The paradox arises again by asking whether this predicate is predicable of itself or not. If so, then it does have the property it attributes, and so is not self predicable; and if not, then it fails to have the property it attributes and so is self predicable. Again, a contradiction. In PM Russell describes seven such paradoxes. One is the "Burali-Forti" paradox concerning the order type of classes of ordinals which had been discovered some years earlier in the emerging mathematical theory of ordinals. The list of seven also includes the paradox of the Liar (concerning the proposition "I am lying"), the Berry paradox of "the least integer not nameable in fewer than nineteen syllables" (which can be named in eighteen), and the related Richard paradox. Finding an adequate solution to these paradoxes constituted the main foundational problem that accompanied the technical details of deriving mathematics in PM.

Around 1907 Russell came to diagnose the paradoxes as arising from violations of the "vicious circle principle" of Poincaré. The paradox of the set of all sets that are not members of themselves Russell then saw as arising from the implicit assumption that the expressions used in characterizing the set are well defined. The paradox is banished if it is seen as requiring an illicit totality, one dependent on itself in a viciously circular fashion. Russell saw similar vicious circles in the other paradoxes. His solution of the paradoxes lies in the theory of types, a formulation of logic that observes the ban on vicious circles. The basic objects of the logic, propositional functions, are to be distinguished into types. There are differences between the type of functions of objects and that of functions of those functions, and so on. That is the hierarchy of what might be called "simple" types. The full type theory, however, is "ramified". There are further differences between the type of a function defined in terms of a quantifier ranging over other functions and the type of those other functions, even though the functions apply to arguments of the same simple type. A function so defined by quantification over functions belongs to a higher type (or "order" to mark this particular distinction of type). The paradox of sets is resolved by first providing the "No-Class" theory, which provides a "logical construction" of classes in terms of propositional functions. The paradoxes of classes are accordingly reduced to violations of the theory of types for functions. The other paradoxes are reduced to violations of type distinctions in various similar ways.

The ramified nature of the theory of types, however, leads immediately to technical difficulties for the project of reducing mathematics to logic. Many common definitions in mathematics seem to violate the vicious circle principle. They include classes of different orders in the range of one quantifier and so seemingly violating the ban on defining a class in terms of a totality to which that class must be seen as belonging. Such "impredicative" definitions are commonplace in mathematical practice. Russell avoids this problem with his "axiom of reducibility". The axiom asserts that for any predicate of given arguments defined by quantifying over higher order functions or classes, there is another coextensive but "predicative"function of the same type of arguments. A predicative function is of lowest possible order compatible with a given type of argument. The existence of this coextensive predicative function is all that is needed for the purposes of set theory and the rest of the extensional notions of mathematics. Yet this principle seems an *ad hoc* addition to the logic, indeed it seems contrary to the vicious circle principle which motivates the whole notion of type. As will be described below, Russell was hesitant about adopting the axiom of reducibility from the beginning. Others have been more harsh in their view of the axiom. A suspicion that the axiom of reducibility undoes the effects of the ramification of types or is even blatantly inconsistent with the rest of the theory has thus dogged the reception of PM since the early 1920s. This issue will be the topic of chapter 6 below.

Aside from questions about the details of the theory of types and orders, how it is motivated by the vicious circle principle, and how to justify the axiom of reducibility, the other major issue of concern with the foundations of the logic of PM is understanding the place of the "multiple relation theory" of judgment in the introduction. There Russell denies the existence of propositions, claiming that symbols for them are "incomplete", just like definite descriptions and class terms. The quantifiers in PM do indeed range only over propositional functions and not propositions (with one frequently noted exception discussed below). Yet surely the notion of a propositional *function*, which is a function from arguments to propositions, presupposes the existence of propositions. How is all this to be reconciled?

Russell's ontological views seem fairly uniform during this period. Throughout Russell accepts a Platonist realm of universals, both monadic and relations of different types and minds, and sense data. There are some changes during this period, however. In the beginning Russell's ontology includes matter as basic, to be known, however, only by inference from our sense data. By the end he wanted to "construct" matter from sense data. Facts are also an important component of the later ontology, but their importance is less clear when they first appear, around 1910 at the end of the composition of PM. Still, however, the ontology seems fairly constant.

It seems natural to ask about the relation of Russell's logical and ontological views. How exactly do propositions and facts relate within the logic? What of propositional functions and universals? Throughout most of this century the notion that logic is deeply involved in ontological commitments of its own has been rejected. Logic has been seen as ontologically neutral, as concerning "topic neutral" principles with which arguments about ontology are to be discussed. Indeed recent views see logic as an uninterpreted formalism awaiting interpretation in some domain before even the quantifiers "for all" and "for some" have a determinate meaning. This more extreme view of logic has also been associated with nominalism about universals. The predicate expressions of logic, for example, are claimed to be schematic letters awaiting interpretation in different ways, rather than constants or variables that denote properties. That interpretation consists of substituting some actual open sentence of an "interpreted" language for the letters. Such resulting "open sentences" are all there is to predication, and, it was suggested, predication was all there was to the problem of universals. This view of logic, expounded by W.V. Quine almost directly as a reaction to what he saw as use/mention confusions in Russell's logic, is not in keeping with Russell's own view of logic. Russell did not view logic as an uninterpreted calculus waiting for many possible interpretations.[4] Rather, for Russell,

---

[4]See Hylton [1980] and Goldfarb [1989], for Russell's view of logic, and Quine [1987] for Quine's alternative.

logic is a single "interpreted" body of *a priori* truths, of propositions
rather than sentence forms. It is, however, maximally general and topic
neutral. In fact, Russell takes the universality of logical principles as
one of their distinguishing characteristics when he wonders whether the
axiom of reducibility belongs in the logic. But he does not treat logic as
an uninterpreted formalism.

My thesis is that Russell's logical and metaphysical views are not only
compatible, but that his metaphysics and logic inform each other. Many
features of Russell's logic can be explained by metaphysical views that he
was expounding at the same time. This thesis has several components.
I will attempt to explain distinctive features of the logic in terms of
the underlying metaphysics. I will also try to defend the view that the
metaphysics did not change as much as has been suggested during the
period from 1908 to 1919 characterized by relatively stable logical views.
It is true that Russell's metaphysical writings follow the composition,
if not the publication, of the technical parts of PM. The introduction
was composed later, as were the most prominent metaphysical writings.
Many interpreters of this period, including Nino Cocchiarella, take the
emerging "logical atomist" metaphysics as a later development, and,
moreover, one that is incompatible with the logic of PM. I argue to the
contrary, that the elements of that atomist logic underly the logic of PM.
The introduction to PM is not a late uneasy addition, but a substantive
exposition of the logical and metaphysical ideas behind the logic. With
further study of Russell's unpublished manuscripts it may turn out that I
am wrong about this chronology. If so, a weaker claim is still defensible,
namely, that the metaphysical theories of this period were motivated
by, or at least compatible with, the logical views. That logic should
be in any way constrained by ontology is another view that seems odd
after the syntactic turn in logic in this century. It certainly is in keeping,
however, with Wittgenstein's *Tractatus Logico-Philosophicus* [1922], and
also, I think, with all of Russell's logical work. If not expounding the
metaphysical views that underlay his logic, Russell was, at the very
least, working out the metaphysical view embedded implicitly in that
logic.

This comparison with the *Tractatus* raises the important question of
the role of Wittgenstein in Russell's thinking in this period. Wittgenstein arrived at Cambridge in October of 1911, the year after the first
volume of PM had appeared. Immediately Wittgenstein and Russell engaged in very deep discussions of that work. Wittgenstein was also very
much aware of the views expressed in *The Problems of Philosophy* [PoP]
(published early in 1912) and was apparently distressed by the book, and
not simply because it was an attempt at popularization. The ontology of

PoP was in fact Russell's considered position. That book should not be read simply as the excellent introductory text in philosophy that it is. It is also a briefer statement of the more developed positions in the unpublished *Theory of Knowledge* manuscript of 1913 that was to be aimed at a professional audience. Russell abandoned that manuscript, perhaps the only piece of writing of that size that he did not see into print. It has become clear that Wittgenstein engaged in extensive discussion of that material with Russell and that his criticisms were largely responsible for Russell giving up the project. It has emerged that Wittgenstein's criticisms of the "multiple relation" theory were the heart of the objections.[5] The effects of those criticisms on Russell's thinking during the war, leading up to the *Philosophy of Logical Atomism* [PLA] lectures of 1918, is a crucial point for the discussion that follows. Some, such as Cocchiarella, see the transition as dramatic. He reads the logical atomism lectures as deeply influenced by Wittgenstein, and the logic that they embrace as an extensional, second order but unramified, logic in the second edition of PM in 1925. Cocchiarella gives the following as his account of Russell's changing views, beginning with a summary of the changes that occurred in 1908 with the first version of the theory of types:

> Classes now were taken as analysable in terms of propositional functions, even though the latter were still construed as nonentities, i.e. as reducible to the many propositions that were their values. Later in 1910, the ontological roles of propositions and propositional functions were reversed: i.e. propositions were then taken to be nonentities while each propositional function was assumed to be (or to have corresponding to it) a real property or relation. This reversal was a consequence of Russell's rejection in 1910 of his earlier theory of belief and judgment (as a relation between a mind and a proposition) in favour of his then new multiple relations theory (as a relation between a mind and the constituents or components of a proposition), which required that propositional functions, but not propositions, be real single entities.
>
> As a result of arguments given by Ludwig Wittgenstein in 1913, Russell, from 1914 on, gave up the Platonistic view that properties and relations could be logical subjects. Predicates were still taken as standing for properties and relations, but only in their role as predicates; i.e., nominalized predicates were no longer allowed as abstract singular terms in Russell's new version of his logically perfect language. Only particu-

---

[5] See Griffin [1985].

lars could be named in Russell's new metaphysical theory, which he called logical atomism, but which, unlike his earlier 1910–1913 theory is a form of natural realism, not logical realism, since now the only real properties and relations of his ontology are simple material properties and relations that are the components of the atomic facts that make up the world. Complex properties and relations in this framework are simply propositional functions, which, along with propositions, are now merely linguistic expressions. (Cocchiarella [1991], 798)

I will present a different account of Russell's logical ontology. This alternative account assumes that while Russell was upset by Wittgenstein's criticisms he did not convert to the position that Wittgenstein was developing. Russell may well have set aside the 1913 manuscript because of Wittgenstein's criticisms and not just because of the distractions of World War I. Russell lost contact with Wittgenstein during the war and developed his own views independently. There are some signs of Wittgenstein's influence in the lectures, however. In particular, Russell credits Wittgenstein with reinforcing the view that predicable entities are of a different type from objects. Cocchiarella thinks that this is a crucial break with the earlier view that propositional functions could be named and thus be the subjects of propositions. That earlier view, Cocchiarella argues, was replaced by an ontology of universals which were distinctively predicable in nature, and could not be named. Cocchiarella's account, I will argue below, does not represent the real relation of propositional functions and universals in Russell's thinking. I hold that the metaphysics of the Logical Atomism lectures is a continuation of the views of 1910 in PoP and of the 1913 manuscript. While disheartened by Wittgenstein's criticisms, Russell was not led by them into a conversion to the view of the *Tractatus*. I think that Russell in fact forged ahead with his thinking, trying to accommodate Wittgenstein's objections, but maintaining the same basic framework.

There was a dramatic shift in Russell's thinking, which was influenced by Wittgenstein, but it did not occur until after World War I. The catalyst for these changes was Frank Ramsey, who had contact with both Russell and Wittgenstein and served as an intermediary between the two. It was Ramsey who influenced Russell to rethink the very nature of logic. To the extent that Russell did, the results were only the introduction to the second edition of PM and three appendices. That introduction undoes many of the major ideas of the first edition. It presents a logic which is extensional and where all higher order sentences are constructed from atomic first order sentences. Logic is seen as formal, and propositional functions thus more susceptible to a nominalist interpretation. Russell went along with this reinterpretation, and later in life, in *My Philosophical Development* [MPD], reads it back into the first edition of PM. In fact, I consider the later Russell to be a very prominent member of the series of misinterpreters of the first edition of PM. Russell probably did not fully appreciate the significance of the many great changes in logic introduced by Wittgenstein and Ramsey. Russell did acknowledge their influence on the second edition, but that influence was not deep. The revisions are just sketched in the new material and the body of the text is untouched.[6] In 1924 Ramsey complained to Wittgenstein that Russell was slow, growing old, and unable to understand the new things the two of them were up to.[7] Wittgenstein cast a spell, changing logic in a dramatic way, so much that earlier logic became incomprehensible for many philosophers. It is only now, with the development of intensional logic and the realist metaphysics of the last few years, that it is possible to rediscover the metaphysical and logical views underlying *Principia Mathematica*. What follows is my attempt at such a rediscovery.

This inclination to read Russell's later metaphysical views back into PM is just one of the temptations the present account seeks to avoid. Another is the tendency to read PM solely from the point of view of Russell's earlier views in *Principles of Mathematics* and the period up to 1908 when he was searching for a solution to the paradoxes. This approach is a natural result of the growth of interest in that early period sparked by the editing of the unpublished papers in the Russell archives. Peter Hylton's *Russell, Idealism, and the Emergence of Analytic Philosophy* [1990] is the most prominent of this group of studies, to which Landini ([1987], [1993], [1996], and [1998]) and Pelham [1993] also belong. Both Pelham and Hylton focus on Russell's metaphysical and logical views from the time of *Principles of Mathematics* and before, through the early reactions to the paradoxes and Russell's abandoned attempts at resolutions before settling on the theory of types. Certain features of Russell's early views are out of keeping with those in PM and later. It is here that I see Russell's views undergoing a significant change. As a result, then, I will insist that the period of 1908–1919 marks a distinctive, but homogenous, period of Russell's metaphysical and logical views, with both the periods before and after marking significant changes that have been mistakenly read into interpretations of works in this period.

---

[6] Even though the text was completely reset, the original plates having been lost.

[7] In a letter from Ramsey to Wittgenstein quoted in Monk ([1990], 219).

One position that was of great importance to Russell from PoM to ML was what has become known as the "doctrine of the unrestricted variable".[8] Part of this doctrine is the view, which soon became standard in logic, that restricted quantification, as in "All Fs are Gs", is to be interpreted by an unrestricted universal quantifier and a conditional: "For everything, if it is F, then it is G". Russell saw this as a criticism of the notion that logical kinds or sorts are fundamental, for even to say that something x only belongs to a certain category is to treat 'x' as an unrestricted variable, ranging over everything. In PoM Russell introduces the expression 'term' this way:

> Whatever may be an object of thought, or may occur in any true proposition, or can be counted as *one*, I call a *term*. This, then, is the widest word in the philosophical vocabulary. I shall use as synonymous with it the words unit, individual, entity. ... A man, a moment, a number, a class, a relation, a chimaera, or anything else that can be mentioned, is sure to be a term; and to deny that such and such a thing is a term must always be false. ([PoM], 43–44)

Because a "mark" of terms is their "identity and diversity", it follows that:

> Numerical identity and diversity are the source of unity and plurality; and thus the admission of many terms destroys monism. And it seems undeniable that every constituent of every proposition can be counted as one, and that no proposition contains less than two constituents. *Term* is, therefore, a useful word, since it marks dissent from various philosophies, as well as because, in many statements, we wish to speak of *any* term or *some* term. ([PoM], 44)

Several themes are drawn together in this last passage. Russell ties his rejection of monism in favor of "realism" to his notion of term. Thus Hylton argues that since 'term' is the widest ontological notion, and since terms are what the quantifiers *any* and *some* range over, it follows that this passage expresses a deep opposition to anything like the later theory of types.[9] Variables must be absolutely unrestricted in their range rather than restricted to a particular logical category. Hence there is an incompatibility between the doctrine of the unrestricted variable and the notion of logical types.

---

[8]See Landini ([1993] and [1998], chapter 10.6) for his discussion of the role of this principle in PM.

[9]Cf. Hylton ([1990], 315 and elsewhere in chapter 7.)

Hylton also finds an extreme atomism to be central to Russell's early views. The terms, which are all distinct, must be related to each other solely by "external" relations. No term depends for its nature on any other. But classifying terms into types does present them as bearing internal relations to each other. If individuals and predicates are of different types, related by the special way a predicate must be completed by an individual to form a proposition, Russell's earlier atomism seems violated. Thus both on the logical ground of abandoning the unrestricted variable, and the metaphysical ground of accepting internal relations, Hylton sees Russell as backsliding, abandoning views that were central to his whole early realist philosophy, without appreciating the extent of this change. He thus hints that there is no coherent realist metaphysics underlying the logic of PM.

Another response to the difference between Russell's views in the earlier period and in PM is to read some of those earlier views into PM. Pelham and Landini [1987], for example, concentrate on Russell's "substitutional" account of propositional functions and see traces of it in PM. In several papers from 1906 to ML, Russell considers an account of logic which acknowledges only propositions and individuals. Propositional functions are seen as "incomplete symbols" or logical constructions on the model of definite descriptions from "On Denoting" [OD]. The notion of one proposition resulting from a substitution in another is taken as basic. The notation for this varies in Russell's notes, but one system has '$p/a; b!q$', for 'p with b substituted for a yields q'. Any statement seemingly about a propositional function must be made indirectly as a claim about the various propositions resulting from substitutions of one term for another in a given proposition. This substitutional account of functions seems to have been abandoned by Russell fairly quickly as he discovered that it led to its own version of the paradoxes. Still, some consider the substitutional account a great influence on Russell's later views in PM.

Pelham, for example, presents the substitutional account as a last attempt to maintain the unrestricted variable. It is not only ordinary individuals that may be substituted in propositions. One can also consider the result of substituting a proposition for something in a proposition. If something does not "occur" as a constituent of a proposition, however, the result of a substitution will be the original proposition, unchanged. Thus the variable can be unrestricted, but have the effect of ranging over individuals alone, provided that no proposition occurs in the target of the substitutions. Pelham sees the mark of the earlier substitutional account in a certain ambivalence towards propositional functions in PM. Predicable entities seem to have a dual role as constituents of propositions and as derived from propositions. Indeed she asserts that Russell attempts to maintain the doctrine of unrestricted variables in PM. The denial of the independent existence of propositional functions in the spirit of the substitutional account is then combined with the denial of the existence of propositions by the "multiple relation" theory, leaving only individuals as genuine entities. I will argue to the contrary, however, that the metaphysical picture underlying the multiple relation theory is a coherent source of both the views about propositions and propositional functions, and is based on a typed ontology.

Landini's views, presented in *Russell's Hidden Substitutional Theory* [1998] and other works, are more radical. He insists that the doctrine of the unrestricted variable is still maintained in PM. Variables seem to be restricted to types, but only when they are not simple and instead have some internal structure which reveals their limitation. These typed expressions are all really metalinguistic, and not genuine variables. Similarly with most of the apparatus of PM, including the quantifiers which should be treated as "substitutional" in the contemporary sense of asserting, metalinguistically, all subsitution instances of the formula that follows. It follows that the lack of a system of type indices in a formalization of PM, seen by many as an oversight to be corrected in their versions, is instead, Landini insists, a sign that apparent (or bound) variables are *not* restricted to types. Types can only apply to schematic formulas and encode metalinguistic information about the truth conditions of certain expressions. In chapter 5 below more of his views will be considered. These include the claims that bound variables for functions only range over predicative functions and that the notation '$\phi\hat{x}$' Russell uses when discussing propositional functions does not represent an abstraction operator, as is assumed by other commentators. One of the driving forces for this novel interpretation of the logic of PM, however, is an attention to the continuities between the earlier substitutional account and the later PM.

Compared with this group, my interpretation of PM will seem backward looking. The work between 1908 and 1919 is a better guide to the logic of PM than the earlier work antedating PM. While Russell's logical views may have been fluid before the theory of types, they jelled into a coherent position in PM and then remained stable for some time. At the same time a metaphysical picture emerged, with, I suggest, many continuities with the realism that Russell had been championing for some time. That new picture was the logical atomist ontology of particulars, universals and facts, replacing the ontology of "platonic atomism" consisting just of propositions that Hylton finds in Russell throughout his earlier period. The new developments in our understanding of Russell's earlier views do not require the revolution in interpretation of the mature views that some would suggest.

UNIVERSALS AND PROPOSITIONAL FUNCTIONS

After Russell rejected his initial idealist views at the end of the 1890s he turned to an atomistic form of realism emphasizing the reality of relations for the rest of his philosophical career. While he was impressed with the possibility of reducing monadic universals to equivalence classes, such as the reduction of colors to classes of similar objects he mentions in *The Problems of Philosophy*, he saw relations as a fundamental category in his ontology. Indeed this commitment to relations preceded his interest in logicism. Russell's work in the years preceding his encounter with Peano at the 1900 World Congress focused on relations and the philosophy of geometry, in which spatial relations were his central interest. Indeed, in an early draft of the *Principles of Mathematics*, before adopting the later "Frege-Russell" account of numbers as equivalence classes of classes, he considered treating numbers as ratios or relations between relations.[1]

This realism about universals continued throughout his career. In the same years that *Principia Mathematica* was appearing (1910–1913) Russell wrote *The Problems of Philosophy*, with its prominent defence of a Platonic realism about relations, and the paper "On the Relations of Universals and Particulars", which considers the possibility of reducing particulars to bundles of universals. Years later, in *My Philosophical Development*, Russell still asserts his belief in universals as something that cannot be reduced to language ([MPD], 174) (although this passage will require more discussion below). This Platonist theory of universals, and in particular, of relations, and the opposition to nominalism, can be seen as a constant throughout Russell's shifting ontological theories.

Yet Russell also said that his whole philosophical career could be described as a "gradual retreat from Pythagoras" ([MPD], 154).[2] It is perhaps significant that he does not describe this as a retreat from *Plato*.

---

[1] In the first surviving version of PoM, the draft of 1899–1900, item **1** in CP3.

[2] See Monk [1996] for discussion of this remark.

Russell never gave up his belief in the reality of relations. Rather he shifted away from his concern with the Pythagorean universe of mathematical entities. He abandoned some abstract entities, most prominently propositions, and always sought to analyze entities as equivalence classes or some other construction of ordinary entities. I think it was that turn to construction in metaphysics, as well as his move from philosophical interests to social reform, education and political activity, that constitute his retreat from Pythagoras. It was not a move from realism to nominalism about universals.

There is a long tradition of interpreting Russell's talk of propositions and propositional functions in a nominalist fashion.[3] That interpretation is encouraged by Russell's own language: "A 'propositional function', in fact, is an expression containing one or more undetermined constituents, such that, when values are assigned to these constituents, the expression becomes a proposition." This statement reappears several times over the years with different wording, as well as the assertion that a proposition is a "form of words which expresses what is true or false".[4] Russell's discussion of propositions or propositional functions as linguistic items cannot be read in the narrowly syntactic fashion of a nominalist. Russell always considers language to be what we would call "interpreted", a piece of language with the meaning it has. Sometimes that meaning is an abstract or Platonic entity, sometimes the meanings are rather the "reference" of singular terms. Russell always resisted Frege's [1892] notion of sense and reference, and so it is accordingly necessary to avoid reading Russell as one who distinguishes a piece of language from its sense as Frege does. A careful look at Russell's remarks about the existence of universals, even much later in MPD (chapter 18), shows that he insists that these entities have some sort of existence, although it is not the same as that of ordinary particulars. Indeed in that later work, part of Russell's resistance to Logical Positivism and Ordinary Language Philosophy is that those movements are too concerned only with language and conventions for its use, ignoring truth conditions and meanings that language has intrinsically. This is the moral of Russell's fable of the restaurateur who insists on calling horse-flesh "beef" ([MPD], 162). When Russell says that an entity is "linguistic", he means that it is the subject matter of logic, and not an ordinary concrete particular. It does not "exist" in the

---

[3]See, for example, Sainsbury [1980] who presents a "substitutional" account of quantification over propositional functions, and Richards [1980] who replies to the nominalist interpretation. Landini [1998] has this nominalist interpretation as the background of his other, more radical views about the ontology of PM.

[4]The first quote is from IMP (155–156), but almost identical phrasings can be found in PM (14) and PLA (202), both quoted below. The latter is from PLA (96).

same sense as ordinary individuals. It is not the piece of uninterpreted syntax that the nominalists would make of it.

Russell did change his mind on major philosophical issues, including some matters of ontology. Propositions disappeared around 1908, as did the self around 1918. Some notions, however, remained constant. At issue below will be the extent to which the metaphysical views of the Logical Atomism period can be read back into the logic of PM. In what follows I will defend the thesis that Russell's atomist metaphysics is at least consistent with his logic. The second edition of PM does not fit well with the views expounded here, however, and given the widespread consequences of adopting the thesis that logic is extensional, it should not be expected that they would. Contra Cocchiarella [1991], it will be argued below that Russell maintained a realist view of sorts towards all three successive categories of universals, propositional functions and propositions, while seeing each category as ontologically dependent on those that precede it.

2.1 UNIVERSALS

Russell was not only a realist about universals; his realism was of the Platonist or "transcendental" variety, to use D.M. Armstrong's [1978] terminology. In general, a universal can be characterized as some one thing that certain similar, but numerically distinct, objects have in common. The "having" here is analyzed in different ways. In the opening lines of the *Categories* Aristotle speaks of things "said of" subjects and "present in" them ([1984], 3). Although scholars may not agree about exactly what distinction is being made, Aristotle's terms nicely characterize a longstanding division between kinds of talk about universals. One line of interest focusses on the relation of particulars to the universals that are somehow "in" or a part of them, the second on the connection between universals and predication. According to that second line universals are what are predicated "of" objects in propositions. Both approaches to universals are present in Russell's thinking, with the notions of particularity and exemplification most prominent in the metaphysical writings, and the notion of predication, of course, in the logical writings.

Armstrong suggests that different theories of universals of my first sort can be distinguished according to their accounts of how a universal inheres in an instance. An *immanent* or Aristotelian theory of universals sees inherence as the spatial relation of location.[5] Universals are located

---

[5] Armstrong [1997] more recently suggests that immanent universals are constituents of their instances which in fact are really states of affairs. One may still

in, or spatially coincident with, their instances. Particulars and universals differ in this, that each particular has a unique spatio-temporal location, while universals can be located in each of many spatially and temporally separated objects. This is not the way that an object can be multiply located, by having different *parts* in different locations, but rather by being *wholly* located in each of their instances. Being multiply located, then, is the distinctive feature of universals.

The *transcendent* or Platonic view of universals that Russell advocates, on the other hand, distinguishes universals from particulars by denying that the former have any spatio-temporal location. In fact Russell speaks of universals as not even 'existing' but rather as 'subsisting', saving the former for what is in space and time.

> ...the relation 'north of' does not seem to *exist* in the same sense in which Edinburgh and London exist. If we ask 'Where and when does this relation exist?' the answer must be 'Nowhere and nowhen'. There is no place or time where we can find the relation 'north of'. It does not exist in Edinburgh anymore than in London, for it relates the two and is neutral between them. Nor can we say that it exists at any particular time. ([PoP], 98)

This passage is surprising, coming from the famous critic of Meinong:

> Thus thoughts and feelings, mind and physical objects *exist*. But universals do not exist in this sense; we shall say that they *subsist* or *have being*, where 'being' is opposed to 'existence' as being timeless. The world of universals, therefore, may also be described as the world of being. The world of being is unchangeable, rigid, exact, delightful to the mathematician, the logician, the builder of metaphysical systems, and all who love perfection more than life. The world of existence is fleeting, vague, without sharp boundaries, without any clear plan or arrangement, but it contains all thoughts and feelings, all the data of sense, and all physical objects, everything that can do either good or harm, everything that makes any difference to the value of life and the world. According to our temperaments, we shall prefer the contemplation of the one or of the other. The one we do not prefer will probably seeem to us a pale shadow of the one we prefer, and hardly worthy to be regarded as in any sense real. But

---

spatially locate universals by their instances, but the inherence relation is the special relation of a constituent to a state of affairs to which it belongs. This still allows a sharp contrast with Platonic realism.

the truth is that both have the same claim on our impartial attention, both are real, and both are important to the metaphysician. ([PoP], 100)

I have suggested that it is the move away from the contemplation of this world of universals that Russell alludes to as his "retreat from Pythagoras", a move from the mysteries of the mathematical world to the world of thought, sensation and matter. It is not a move to nominalism and away from Platonism about relations. Instead, Russell held on to his version of Plato's "theory of ideas" throughout his philosophical career.

One serious challenge for any such transcendental Platonism is to give an account of the relation between concrete particulars and those transcendental universals. In fact Armstrong claims that this is a weakness of Platonist realism. He asserts that any account of this relation leads to a vicious infinite regress. Universals must be related to their instances by a relation, but some relation must relate that relation to the instances, and so on. Plato spoke of objects "participating in" or "copying" the forms. Armstrong claims that Platonists persist with such metaphorical accounts of a relation and that this persistence leads to catastrophe. Instead, he suggests, the immanent realist can gloss the "participation" by saying the universals are spatially "in" the instances and then deny that "being in" is some new relation which does not just supervene on the objects and properties that they have. My interest here, however, is not in defending transcendental or Platonist realism, but in identifying the view and using it to characterize Russell's realism.

The second traditional approach to universals, which focusses on their connection with predication, begins with a consideration of the characterizing feature of universals: they are the "ways" things are. Universals, on this approach, are that which is predicated, or "said of", other things. This characterization of universals leads many directly to nominalism, for it would seem that what is "said of" something is a linguistic entity, the sort of thing that can be said rather than the referent of something which is said. Nominalists can be seen, then, as first identifying universals as that which is predicated of or said of other things and then identifying that with bits of language. The relevant piece of language is the portion of sentences from which the singular term has been removed. Put simply, universals are predicates. The relation between a universal and a particular is that of a bit of language to the many things of which it is true, "predicated of", or even, "names" (if one holds that general terms are terms that name many individuals). Conversely, an object "satisfies" or "is characterized by" the predicate.

Viewed from this nominalist position it is easy to see the Platonist as mistaken in treating universals as real entities that serve as the meanings of predicates. Universals then come from "reifying" some linguistic entity or feature. This is exactly how Quine sees the propositional functions of Russell's logic.[6] In his discussions of Russell, Quine indifferently characterizes propositional functions as "meanings" and "universals", criticizing them as ontologically suspect because of their intensionality. Two meanings could be true of the same entities, and so have the same extension, but not be identical. That is acceptable if it is predicates that are said of objects. Linguistic items have clear identity conditions other than their extensions, but intensional entities, like meanings, do not.

As a result of a general prejudice in favor of nominalism in twentieth century logic, and on the basis of loose use of terminology by Russell himself, some have identified the propositional functions of Russell's logic with predicates directly.[7] This is a third possible account of the metaphysics of propositional functions, and seems quite out of keeping with the rest of Russell's realist metaphysics. Some of the passages leading to this interpretation will be important in distinguishing the role of propositional functions and universals, and so will be discussed briefly.

2.2   PROPOSITIONAL FUNCTIONS

Propositional functions are introduced in the *Philosophy of Logical Atomism* lectures as follows:

> A *propositional function* is simply *an expression containing an undetermined constituent, or several undetermined constituents, and becoming a proposition as soon as the undetermined constituents are determined.* If I say 'x is a man' or 'n is a number', that is a propositional function; so is any formula of algebra, say $(x + y)(x - y) = x^2 - y^2$. A propositional function is nothing, but, like most of the things one wants to talk about in logic, it does not lose its importance through that fact. ([PLA], 202)

Later Russell expands on what he means by saying that propositions are "nothing".

> One purpose that has run through all that I have said, has been the justification of analysis, i.e. the justification of logical atomism, of the view that you can get down in theory, but not in practice, to ultimate simples, out of which the

---

[6] "Logic and the Reification of Universals" Quine ([1961], 123).

[7] See Sainsbury [1980] and even Russell himself comes close to this when looking back over his work in MPD (chapter 6 and 174), discussed above.

world is built, and that those simples have a kind of reality
not belonging to anything else. Simples, as I tried to explain,
are of an infinite number of sorts. There are particulars and
qualities and relations of various orders, a whole hierarchy of
different sorts of simples, but all of them, if we were right,
have in their various ways some kind of reality that does not
belong to anything else. The only other sort of object you
come across in the world is what we call *facts*, and facts are
the sort of things that are asserted or denied by propositions, and are not properly entities at all in the same sense
in which their constituents are. That is shown by the fact
that you cannot name them. You can only deny, or assert, or
consider them, but you cannot name them because they are
not there to be named, although in another sense it is true
that you cannot know the world unless you know the facts
that make up the truths of the world; but the knowing of
facts is a different sort of thing from the knowing of simples.
([PLA], 234–235)

Facts are clearly basic entities in Russell's ontology; they are not "logical constructions". Yet they are "not properly entities" either, he says,
because they are not nameable. Russell says that under Wittgenstein's
influence he had come to see the significance of the difference in logical
type between individuals and propositions ([PLA], 182). Only individuals can, properly speaking, be named. Propositions are of a different
logical type. Propositions can only be asserted or judged. If we then read
this logical difference as revealing a metaphysical distinction, as Russell
seems to have done, we will say that individuals, the things that can be
named, have a primary kind of existence. The existence of facts is of a
different category or logical type. This difference of type, I believe, also
explains the remarks that propositional functions are "nothing". Russell
stresses the difference of type between functions and individuals. Propositional functions are not individuals, namely, of the lowest logical type,
but they do not lose "importance through that fact". Propositions are
not *properly* entities, in virtue of belonging to a different logical type
than the real, or basic individuals in the world.[8]

The suggestion that propositional functions are merely predicates and
that the quantifiers of PM are thus "substitutional" draws its support
from two kinds of sources: the remarks about propositional functions
as nothing and remarks about propositions as linguistic entities. The

---

[8]Cf. Sainsbury [1980] where a nominalist interpretation of propositional functions
is drawn from these same passages.

nominalist tinge to so many passages in Russell can, however, only be attributed to a lack of interest in language, rather than to simple use/mention confusions. Russell can be quite explicit about the distinction when he cares to observe it. At PM (44) he says that a " 'proposition' (in the sense in which this is to be distinguished from the phrase expressing it) is not a single entity at all". Similarly, we should read the above passage about propositional functions becoming propositions when certain constituents are determined as an indicator that functions are more similar to propositions than to sentences. A propositional function falls short of being a proposition by the absence of an argument. The constituents of propositions are all real objects, not linguistic symbols, and so propositional functions should be seen as entities, not symbols.

Quine takes the quantification over propositional functions in PM and other realist talk to indicate that functions are meant to be other than just symbols, and in particular, that the quantifications involves one in a commitment to abstract entities. Propositional functions are meanings, what predicates stand for. But also, for Quine, they are universals, and so he identifies propositional functions in their realist form as universals. Even this identification of propositional universals and functions, so construed, will not do, however. A further distinction must be made.

The evidence that Russell had two sorts of general or universal entities in his ontology is indirect, for he does not ever explicitly distinguish the two. More importantly, on the other hand, he doesn't explicitly identify them either. He does not speak, as one might suppose he would had he made such an identification, of his logic of propositional functions as providing an understanding of universals.[9] He does not identify propositional functions as the successors to universals, what universals have become through developments of modern logic. He does talk of how modern mathematics has tamed infinite and natural numbers by reducing them to classes. But not so for universals. Russell never proposes a "logicist" account of universals. Passages where he might seem to identify functions and universals should be read carefully. He does talk, for instance, of what entities predicates *stand for* and identifies those as universals ([MPD], 175). In that particular passage, he is responding to Quine's doubts about allowing any second order quantification that does not really reduce to either quantification over sets or substitutional quantification over predicates. Both propositional functions and universals were real for Russell; both would make him a realist in the eyes of a nominalist, like Quine, so both are things that predicates stand for.

---

[9] But see MPD (175) where he refers to quantification over propositional functions as in "Napoleon had all the qualities of a great general" as raising a question about the existence of universals. Here he comes close to identifying the two.

Attributing a tacit view to so open and transparent a philosopher as Russell requires justification. My project is to not attribute inconsistency or rapid changes of mind unless absolutely necessary. What is left then is a charge of oversight on Russell's part. Russell had two rather distinct lines of investigation concerning predication. One was the metaphysical investigations of universals, and in particular relations, that was the basis of his realist position. The other line was his work in logic. In the early years after his turn to realism, Russell developed the rough outlines of his metaphysical position, and even many of the ideas in PoM, before he had even encountered symbolic logic in the person of Giuseppe Peano at the 1900 World Congress of Philosophy.[10] When working on metaphysics, Russell would think of universals; when working on logic, his focus was on propositional functions. When combining the two, as in the introduction to PM, he did have an idea of how they fit together, but such mixed occasions were rare. As is seen from the later history of PM, the theory of types can be treated formally without even clearly identifying it as a realist system, much less as one involving a commitment to universals. Russell himself never explicitly worked out the metaphysical foundations of his logic, and so that is left for us to do. My proposal attributes only marginal consciousness on Russell's part to the distinction between universals and propositional functions. As such it can be rejected as a reconstruction, or an attempt to impose a consistent position where none was originally there. If so, this proposal is wrong, but it is attempted in the spirit of Russell's [1900] own account of Leibniz's philosophy, and might be excused as a characteristically Russellian error.

My argument will rely on two kinds of evidence: first, puzzles about Russell's account of propositional functions that arise if they are simply identified with universals, and second, on differences between what Russell says about universals when they are characterized as such and when he is explicitly talking about propositional functions. Indeed, that contexts can be easily classified as concerning either universals or propositional functions, and that there are no contexts where the two are used interchangably, is part of the evidence for the distinction. Though Russell might seem to use the terms 'quality', 'property' and 'predicate' interchangably, some distinctions do emerge in their use. The terms 'quality' and 'predicate' are almost always used to refer to universals, while 'property' refers to propositional functions.

---

[10]The writings in CP3, including a substantial first draft of *Principles of Mathematics*, show the extent to which Russell had developed his philosophical position before he encountered Peano's symbolic logic in 1900. See my review of that volume, B. Linsky [1996].

Together, two sections in the introduction to PM present the first puzzle. In successive sections (II and III of Chapter II) of the introduction to the first edition Russell seems first to deny and then to require the existence of propositional functions.[11] In section II Russell argues that the vicious circle principle leads to a classification of propositional functions into different types in this fashion: if propositional functions do not differ in type from their arguments then a propositional function $\phi\hat{x}$ could be applied to itself $\phi(\phi\hat{x})$. This self predication, he claims, would violate the vicious circle principle, according to which an object cannot presuppose a totality to which it belongs. Russell defines a propositional function as follows:

> By a 'propositional function' we mean something which contains a variable x, and expresses a *proposition* as soon as a value is assigned to x. That is to say, it differs from a proposition solely by the fact that it is ambiguous: it contains a variable of which the value is unassigned. ([PM], 38)

Now to read Russell as a realist about propositional functions one must make sense of the "ambiguity" above, as more than linguistic, and also, it would seem, regard variables as constituents of propositions. Throughout the writings from 1910 to 1918 one finds discussions of logical entities such as logical forms and logical constants as real objects. It is this notion that Wittgenstein [1922] is reacting to at *Tractatus* 5.4: "There are no logical objects".[12]

What is important for the current issue is that propositional functions are defined in terms of propositions. Propositions are in some sense prior to propositional functions. Russell explains why the vicious circle principle then implies that functions cannot apply to themselves:

> That is to say a function is not well-defined unless all its values are already well-defined. It follows from this that no function can have among its values anything which presupposes that function, for if it had, we could not regard the objects ambiguously denoted by the function as definite, while conversely as we have seen, the function cannot be definite until its values are definite. ([PM], 39)

---

[11]These sections were composed together in the original version of this part of the introduction, a paper called "The Theory of Logical Types" ([CP6], 3–40), published first in French translation in May of 1910 and then revised by Russell and Whitehead for inclusion in the introduction to PM. (See the textual note at ([CP6], 495). Claims that the two sections are blatantly incompatible, or that one is an afterthought, would go against the history of this text.

[12]See Richards [1980] for a discussion of variables as constituents of propositions and a response to the linguistic reading of Russell.

Some have seen this argument as an egregious example of Russell's allegedly numerous use-mention confusions.[13] Chihara ([1973], 27) argues that Russell must rely on an equivocation. Seeing a propositional function like ($\hat{x}$ is a man) as a piece of language, says Chihara, would make self-predication into a meaningless piece of language: 'is a man is a man'. Viewing propositional functions as entities, Chihara says, makes coherent, if perhaps false, the application of a function to itself: '($\hat{x}$ is a man) is a man'. The latter alternative is indeed Russell's view, the claimed incoherence or circularity in the application of a function to itself is not the superficial incoherence of putting a predicate in the grammatical location of a singular term. Rather the argument is that there is a (metaphysical) circularity in the purported proposition that results from applying a propositional function to itself, an incoherence in the dependency relation between a function and its values. This feature of propositions has gone unnoticed, resulting in many of the charges of use-mention confusions in Russell. Propositions contain their arguments as constituents and so have features that seem to reflect the constituents of language with which they are described.

Russell concludes that all functions, that is to say, propositional functions, presuppose the totality of their values. The converse dependence does not hold:

> It is sufficiently obvious, in any particular case, that a value of a function does not presuppose the function. Thus for example the proposition 'Socrates is human' can be perfectly apprehended without regarding it as the value of the function '$\hat{x}$ is human'. ([PM], 39)

In section II, then, propositional functions presuppose, or at least in some way depend on their values, namely propositions.

The very next section seems to reverse this priority. Russell briefly surveys the "multiple relation" theory of judgment discussed in Chapter XII of the *Problems of Philosophy* and several other writings of the period. This summary begins with the assertion that:

> The Universe consists of objects having various qualities and standing in various relations. ([PM], 43)

But this ontology does not contain propositions:

> Owing to the plurality of objects in a single judgment, it follows that what we call a 'proposition' (in the sense in which this is distinguished from the phrase expressing it) is not a single entity at all. That is to say, the phrase which expresses

---

[13]For example, Chihara ([1973], 27) and Wang ([1974], 115).

a proposition is what we call an 'incomplete symbol'; it does not have meaning by itself, but requires some supplementation in order to acquire a complete meaning. ([PM], 44)

How can propositional functions *depend* in some way on propositions if symbols for propositions are themselves incomplete and the real constituents of the world are qualities, relations and particulars? If propositional functions are just universals then we would have the priority of propositions and propositional functions reversed in successive sections of the introduction. Two different interpretations have been given for these passages.

Cocchiarella ([1980], 102) argues that Russell wavered over the priority of propositions and functions throughout the period after *Principles of Mathematics* and that section III is the official view of PM, with section II as a throwback to an earlier view. The conflict is thus avoided by identifying propositional functions with the constituents into which propositions are to be analyzed. According to Cocchiarella, the multiple relation theory, although a late development, is still the official view of PM. The constituents of propositions, however, include propositional functions. Propositional functions are still propositional or logical in nature, and, for Cocchiarella, it is only that which makes Russell say that they depend on propositions. There are thus two kinds of dependence that can run in opposite directions. Propositional functions are constituents of propositions, making propositions depend on them in one sense, but on the other hand propositional functions can depend on propositions in the other sense, because propositional functions are inherently predicative. Identifying propositional functions and universals thus seems to require bifurcating Russell's notion of dependence. Alonzo Church ([1984], 513) suggests, rather, that section III may be a later addition to PM, and is the first indication of an interest in the multiple relation theory and not really compatible with the logic of PM.[14]

The interpretation I have proposed increases the ontology but maintains a uniform notion of dependence throughout Russell's thinking, one which makes a complex depend on its constituents and a function on its values. If we sharply distinguish universals and propositional functions one can see Russell as at least *trying* to maintain the following coherent picture over the two sections: propositional functions do presuppose a totality of propositions, which in turn presuppose universals and particulars.

---

[14]See footnote 10 above, however, for the history of the composition of the introduction.

The second puzzle for the identification of propositional functions and universals is a seeming conflict between the vicious circle principle and Russell's platonic realism about universals. Russell formulates the vicious circle principle with different terminology in different places.[15] One statement of the principle is this:

> If, provided a certain collection had a total, it would have members only definable in terms of that total, then the said collection has no total. ([PM], 37)

It has been pointed out by a series of commentators, including Ramsey [1965], Gödel ([1944], 456), and Quine ([1966], 127), that there is no obvious justification for applying this principle to entities that exist prior to, or independently of, any act of definition. Of course an expression cannot be properly defined in terms of itself. It seems odd, however, to speak of *objects* as definable. A definite description such as 'the tallest person in the room' identifies an individual in terms of a totality (the people in the room) to which he or she belongs, and the 'tallest' can *only* be defined by such reference. It is only if the object is somehow created by the definition that such a prohibition might apply. There thus seems to be a *constructivist* element in the account of propositional functions which is out of step with the Platonic realism of the theory of universals. Again, distinguishing propositional functions from universals will resolve the incongruity.

The lack of an account of our knowledge of universals is usually a weak point of a Platonic realism; however, the account of our epistemic access to the world is in fact a central part of Russell's theory. He holds that we are *acquainted* with the objects of sensation, or sense data, but also bear this very same epistemic relation to universals. This relation of acquaintance is also the basis of Russell's theory of meaning:

> Every proposition which we can understand must be composed wholly of constituents with which we are acquainted. ([PoP], 58)

Much attention has been focused on questions about the *particulars* that can be constituents of "Russellian" propositions. Are they sense data or ordinary objects, and how do "logically proper names" refer to these constituents? For Russell, however, most particulars will be known only by description and so the propositions about them will be composed almost entirely of universals with which we are acquainted. It

---

[15] Using the notion of what a bound variable *involves* in OI (198), what a collection *involves* at PM (37) and what is assuming that a set has a total *presupposes*, in ML (155).

is only by *analysis*, using for example the theory of descriptions, that we can discover the genuine constituents of propositions, acquaintance with which is necessary in order to understand those propositions. There are some universals that we know only by description, just as with particulars. But acquaintance is possible with some. Russell tentatively lists those things with which we are acquainted as "... sensible qualities, relations of space and time, similarity, and certain abstract logical universals" ([PoP], 109). Determining the inventory of "logical universals" with which we are acquainted, including the candidate "logical forms", was a central problem of the *Theory of Knowledge* manuscript. These logical universals later became a target of Wittgenstein's criticisms. If universals can be known both by acquaintance and description, they are epistemologically on a par with sense data, which does not fit with their being simply linguistic entities. Universals are not simply *meanings* if a meaning is something that is automatically acquired with a grasp of proper linguistic usage. Rather universals are non linguistic entities, acquaintance with which is required for understanding.

Russell says that the phrases which express propositions are "incomplete symbols". He later calls things so expressed "logical constructions". His claim should be taken to mean that the symbols for propositions are incomplete symbols. Talk of propositions is to be analysed with expressions standing for the particulars and universals which are the real objects of judgment, the same particulars and universals with which we must be acquainted if we are to understand sentences. For example, understanding the sentence 'Socrates is human' requires acquaintance with the universal *humanity* (or rather the constituents of the ultimate analysis of 'humanity') and the constituents of the analysis of 'Socrates'. (Since Socrates is known to us only by description as 'the person who is such and such ...' these will be mostly purely qualitative universals as well.)

Propositional functions, however, are in turn constructed out of propositions. A propositional function should be seen as a fragment abstracted from a proposition; it is what remains of the proposition when one or more arguments are removed. We might express such a view by identifying a propositional function with a set of propositions which differ from each other only in a certain position. Thus ($\hat{x}$ is human) might be identified with the set consisting of the propositions *Socrates is human, Aristotle is human*, etc., or rather with the class of ordered pairs of such objects and the representations of the propositions containing them, as in the standard representation of functions as sets of ordered pairs of arguments and values:

$\{\langle$Socrates,$\langle$Socrates,humanity$\rangle\rangle$, $\langle$Aristotle,$\langle$Aristotle,humanity$\rangle\rangle$,...$\}$.

(Notice that the argument reappears as a constituent of the proposition which is the value of the function.)[16] Of course Russell could not use this particular construction, since he wanted to reduce talk of sets or classes to talk of propositional functions via his "no-class" theory . Russell does not say what sort of analysis of propositional functions he would provide. In the case of propositions he only provides an analysis of some contexts in which expressions for them occur, namely, those of the form 'x judges that aRb'. So Russell does not provide a complete contextual definition, nor does it appear that one could do so, if that meant providing an analysis of all occurrences of propositional variables and constants.

Russell says that a propositional function "ambiguously denotes" its values ([PM], 39). Like those other denoting expressions, definite descriptions, the role of a function is to denote something indirectly, not directly in the fashion of logically proper name. Before 1905 Russell held that denoting expressions such as 'The F' and 'Any F' stood for special denoting concepts which either uniquely or ambiguously denote their instances. The theory of OD allowed Russell to describe definite descriptions as "incomplete" symbols not standing for any separate concept at all. Propositional functions share this feature of denoting, but, of course, no contextual definition in terms of a logic based on propositional functions could be provided. Like variables, which are also essentially ambiguous, propositional functions have the derived, or "constructed" role of denoting something else, without being eliminable with a contextual definition. Like denoting concepts, propositional functions seem to lie "between being and nonbeing" (L. Linsky [1987], 36).

Propositional functions are thus constructions out of constructions. They are constructions of, and thus dependent on, propositions, which are in turn constructed from particulars and universals. This account resolves the first puzzle above. Propositional functions do depend on their values, propositions, and so the vicious circle principle can be invoked to argue that no propositional function can have itself as an argument. But propositions themselves are constructed out of particulars and universals

---

[16] See Anderson ([1989], 81–82) for how propositional functions differ from arbitrary functions from objects to propositions. These differences are captured by the notion that both the argument and propositional function contribute constituents to the value of the propositional function. Thus Socrates is a constituent of the value of any propositional function applied to Socrates, and humanity is a constituent of the value of the function $\hat{x}$ is human. Anderson interprets Gödel ([1944], 131n10) as proposing such a model of propositional functions.

and so are dependent on those particulars and universals. If universals are not identified with propositional functions there is no circle of dependence.

Second, the constructivist overtones of the vicious circle principle make sense on this account. Propositional functions *are* constructed entities; they are not among the fundamental constituents of the world, (i.e., the universals and particulars), but rather depend on them at two removes. Russell is not a "constructivist", however. Propositional functions are not the creations of human minds. One should think of this notion of construction as a metaphysical relation; what is constructed is dependent or supervenient on the ultimate entities. This constitutes a proposal about the ontological status of the entities involved. As Jung (1994) points out, the vicious circle principle should be seen as a metaphysical analogue to the axiom of foundation in set theory, both principles asserting that there can be no circular dependencies among objects.[17] It makes sense to think of propositional functions as having a unique ontological analysis which will be subject to the vicious circle principle.

Besides the indirect evidence for distinguishing propositional functions and universals based on these puzzles about dependency, there is some more direct evidence. Russell has an unrestricted comprehension principle for propositional functions. Subject only to type constraints (which are really constraints on what is well formed), every predicate corresponds with a propositional function. There do not seem to be nearly that many universals. The thrust of Russell's metaphysics seems to be towards a fairly "sparse" theory of universals. "Red" and "blue" are standard examples that Russell gives of perceptual qualities. '$\hat{x}$ is red' and '$\hat{x}$ is blue' are propositional functions. Russell says that a finite disjunction of propositional functions is also a propositional function, thus, presumably, '$\hat{x}$ is red or $\hat{x}$ is blue' ([PM], 56). But is there a universal of *being red or being blue*? Russell does not discuss complex disjunctive *universals* such as this one, nor would he have use for them. We do not need to be acquainted with such a universal to understand any proposition. Just being acquainted with red and blue and the logical form of disjunction would suffice for understanding any proposition of which the disjunctive propositional function is a part. Perceptual experience also only requires acquaintance with the simple universals. For

---

[17]Indeed the metaphor of "construction" is used in the account of the Iterative Conception of Set. Sets are thought of as constructed at various "stages" by iteration of the operation of taking the power set or set of all subsets of a given set. Yet this conception is intended as a Platonistic "intended model" for set theory, not a description of human constructions. See chapter 7 below.

Russell, experience is atomistic, composed of sense data of particular experiences of sensory qualities related to each other in different spatial and temporal ways, but not logically related, as by disjunction. Complex disjunctive universals would be compatible with Russell's epistemology if they were known by descriptions such as 'the universal exemplified by all things that are either red or blue', but this seems to run against the whole thrust of Russell's commitment to analysis. It is only by finding the constituents of fully analysed propositions that we find the entities that those propositions really involve. Discussion of 'being red or blue' just seems to beg a logical analysis.

Russell's remark that "... 'Socrates is human' can be perfectly apprehended without regarding it as a value of the propositional function '$\hat{x}$ is human'" ([PM], 39) suggests another difference with respect to analysis between propositional functions and universals. Understanding the proposition does require acquaintance with universals, including, presumably, *humanity*. Indeed, he says quite explicitly, "It should be remembered that a function is not a constituent in one of its values: thus for example the function "$\hat{x}$ is human" is not a constituent of the proposition "Socrates is human" ([PM], 54–55). A relational proposition aRb will have alternative analyses in terms of propositional functions, $\hat{x}Rb$ or $aR\hat{x}$, or even as a relational function $\hat{x}R\hat{y}$ and the arguments a and b. Still, only one universal appears in this proposition, the relation R, and so the proposition will only have one analysis into particulars and a single (relational) universal. The analysis of a proposition in terms of arguments and propositional functions, then, is different from its analysis in terms of particulars and universals.

Propositional functions cannot appear as constituents of propositions as universals do, according to the proposed interpretation. Cocchiarella's contrary account requires that they do. He points out that propositional functions do seem to play the role of constituents in Russell's analysis of 'Napoleon had all the predicates that make a great general' ([PM], 56). (In this context Russell has defined a 'predicate' as a predicative propositional function.) A judgment that Napoleon had all the predicates that make a great general should have at least one second order propositional function as a constituent, namely '$\phi!\hat{x}$ is a predicate required in a great general.' I suggest, rather, that the official position in *PM* is that such propositional functions will disappear in the ultimate analysis of the proposition and so are not among its ultimate constituents. Cocchiarella disagrees. He says that "... whereas the propositional functions that occur in a judgment are indeed 'fragmented' in the sense of analysis, nevertheless, each propositional function, as well as the 'fragments' of that function that result upon analysis, retains its status in the judgment as a single entity" ([1980], 108). To save the identification of propositional functions and universals one must bifurcate the remainder of the theory. There are now two notions of "fragmentation" to add to the two notions of dependence required earlier. How can a propositional function be a constituent in some sense but not in the "ultimate" sense of analysis? I argue simply that functions are not constituents, although they seem to appear in the logical form of propositions before those forms are totally analysed.

On my view propositional functions are analysable even though they are the values of bound variables. The quotation from Cocchiarella above is part of a reply to this passage from Alonzo Church:

> They [Russell and Whitehead] seem to be aware that this fragmenting of propositions requires a similar fragmenting of propositional functions. But the contextual definition or definitions that are implicitly promised by the 'incomplete symbol' characterisation are never fully supplied, and it is in particular not clear how they would explain away the use of bound propositional and functional variables. ([1976], 748)

These proposed "constructions" of propositions from universals and then of propositional functions from propositions are not like other examples of "incomplete symbols". Russell gives contextual definitions allowing the elimination of definite descriptions and class terms from all contexts in which they might occur. Other than some particular examples of analyses of judgments of atomic propositions by the "multiple relation" theory, Russell gives no clue as to how the eliminations will go. As will be discussed below, this is understandable. Propositional functions are central to Russell's logic and must be treated as constituting the range of real, bound, variables. They could not be eliminated in terms of quantifiers over anything else. But that does not mean that the metaphysical notion of analysis and constituents does not apply to them. It is convenient when Russell is able to provide definitions of constructed "entities", but not essential to the notion of construction and dependence.

A search through Russell's writings for an explicit statement of a distinction between universals and propositional functions will be disappointing. His choice of terminology also provides no direct evidence for my thesis, and might even seem inconsistent with it in a few instances. In general, when Russell is clearly discussing universals, he uses the term 'quality', as when he speaks of the world consisting of 'objects having various qualities and standing in various relations' ([PM], 56). In the passage cited above Russell first gives his example as 'Napoleon had all the qualities of a great general' but immediately paraphrases it in terms of 'predicates', suggesting that the ordinary sentence is properly rephrased in technically accurate language. The term 'property' is used in different ways. At PM (166) it is defined: "A 'property of x' may be defined as a propositional function satisfied by x". This is compatible with the definition of 'predicate' in the discussion of the Napoleon example: "If we call a *predicate* of an object a predicative function which is true of that object, then the predicates of an object are only some among its properties". On the next page the axiom of reducibility is characterized as asserting that "... every property belongs to the same collection of objects as is defined by some predicate" ([PM], 57). In all these passages 'property' clearly identifies propositional functions. Elsewhere, however, Russell does seem to suggest that "properties" and "qualities" amount to the same thing: "... speaking generally, adjectives and common nouns express qualities or properties of single things, whereas prepositions and verbs tend to express relations between two or more things' ([PoP], 94). It should be noted, however, that in this passage the "properties" are expressed by *single* words rather than whole phrases, so even this passage is not a blanket identification of qualities and properties. I will argue below that atomic predicates consisting of a variable, copula, and single adjective or verb, as in '$\hat{x}$ is blue', stand directly for a propositional function, while the adjectives or verbs, such as 'blue', stand for universals. In general then, Russell seems to reserve the term 'quality' for talking about universals and 'property' for propositional functions, 'predicate' being reserved for predicative propositional functions. Such a lack of precision in terminology, and the lack of any explicit discussion of the relation of universals and propositional functions is, I think, only explainable by the fact that Russell himself did not adequately work out how universals were to fit into the theory of types.

2.3   UNIVERSALS AND TYPES

If universals are to be distinguished from propositional functions, then do they yet play any role in the theory of types? If type differences do not apply to universals it would seem that universals should all be individuals of the same *logical* category of particulars. This might seem the appropriate view to hold if universals are somehow constituents *in* objects, entirely distinct from the predicable entities *said of* things. Thus while ontologically distinct from particulars, universals would not differ from them in logical treatment. There might well be properties of properties (second order universals), which differ from first order universals, and so on, but that would not be a logical distinction of type. Treating universals as objects would also be natural if PM is viewed as an uninterpreted calculus ready to represent many different ontological views. One such application will be to a metaphysical theory of objects and universals, but another, such as the nominalist story, would also have to be representable. Indeed Russell does consider alternative ontologies, including the possibility of reducing particulars to universals in RUP, without suggesting that any would violate the theory of types.

However, while to some degree topic neutral and surely universally applicable as a logic, the system of PM has an intended interpretation. It does not include symbols awaiting interpretation, but rather is *the* unique and correct logical theory. In this section I will first argue that Russell held particulars and universals to be of different logical types or that he at least came to hold this view very soon after PM, indeed as early as 1913 with ToK. I conclude by arguing that this view is compatible with the views of PM, but only at a certain cost to the universality of PM's language. The type hierarchy seems to apply to both propositional functions and universals, and both hierarchies have a common grounding in a metaphysical view about the particulars and universals that make up the world and how other constructed entities depend on them. In addition to furthering my overarching project of examing the relation between Russell's logic and his ontology, this discussion is important as a rearguard action in establishing the distinction between functions and universals. When Russell says that universals differ in type it is important to demonstrate that he is not doing so because they are simply functions that come in types. It is also important not to go to the other extreme and follow Cocchiarella's interpretation that Russell abandoned an ontology of functions in favor of universals, thus leaving universals to inherit the classification into types. I will hold that both universals and propositional functions are typed.

First, the evidence that universals differ in type from particulars. This is most explicit in the 1913 manuscript *Theory of Knowledge*. In that work the terms 'predicate' and 'relation' clearly stand for universals ([ToK], 80–81).[18] It should also be remembered that Russell spoke of 'terms' where we would speak of the referent of a linguistic term; terms were objects designated by pieces of language. Russell is explicit about the difference of type between universals and particulars: "... subject and predicate obviously differ logically ... Such terms as white, painful, etc., seem to demand subjects in just the same sort of way as relations demand terms." Also, "... subjects and predicates belong to different

---

[18]So if Cocchiarella's account described in chapter 1 of this book is right, the big shift in ontology from functions to universals would have occured at this point immediately after PM.

logical divisions" ([ToK], 90). Thus white is of a different *logical* division from the terms (particulars) to which it applies.

By the time of his two works on logical atomism, "Logical Atomism" [LA] and PLA, Russell is quite explicit: "The statement concerning any particular that it is not a universal is quite strictly nonsense – not false, but strictly and exactly nonsense. You can never place a particular in the sort of place where a universal ought to be, and vice versa" ([PLA], 225). In the 1924 essay, LA, we find: "All words are of the same logical type ... But the meanings are of various different types; an attribute (expressed by an adjective) is of a different type from the objects to which it can be (whether truly or falsely) attributed ... " ([LA], 168). And finally, Russell invokes the difference between types to dispell Bradley's regress: "the conception of the relation (between two terms) as a third term between the other two sins against the doctrine of types, and must be avoided with the utmost care" ([LA], 171). It seems, then, that Russell sees universals to be of different types at this point. These quotes primarily refer to the difference between particulars and (first order) universals, but nothing in them suggests that there are no higher order universals.

An explicit discussion of such qualities of qualities as *second order* universals would be conclusive evidence that universals come in types, but such are not to be found. There are, however, many passages that strongly suggest this view. PM does contain one reference to a "relation between concepts" ([PM], 45). There are also some hints of this view in works contemporaneous with PM. Thus; "Predication is a relation involving fundamental logical difference between two terms. Predicates may themselves have predicates, but the predicates of predicates will be radically different from the predicates of substances" ([RUP], 123). Also note the following from "Knowledge by Acquaintance and by Description" ([KAD], 154): "We are aware of the universal *yellow*; this universal is the subject in such judgments as 'yellow differs from blue' or 'yellow resembles blue less than green does'".

The best evidence that Russell held the view that universals are of different types comes from later writings by others, who maintain that Russell abandoned that view with the second edition of PM. Many think that Russell's logical atomism and his extensional second edition of PM have no place for second order universals.[19] Somehow Russell's talk of universals as essentially predicative is supposed to lead to the consequence that there are no higher order universals. Ramsey, for example, felt that it was a natural consequence of the extensional viewpoint, by which

---

[19] See Cocchiarella [1987], "Russell's Theory of Logical Types and the Atomistic Hierarchy of Sentences".

a propositional function "enters into" a proposition only "through" its values, that all apparent second order predications would be eliminable by paraphrase. To hold that universals are inherently predicative, however, certainly does not require that there be no higher order universals. The use of abstracts for propositional functions, for example, seems to both observe type distinctions and to allow for higher level predication, thus: $\phi(F\hat{x})$. If one sees the circumflexed variable as bound by a (term forming) operator, then that expression both represents the predicative nature of the function and treats the function as the subject of a sentence. The abandonment of higher order universals is perhaps in keeping with the claim that universals are essentially predicative, but not logically required by the view.

Ramsey does attribute to Russell the view that the sentence 'Unpunctuality is a fault', which apparently attributes a second order quality of being a fault to the first order quality of being unpunctual, really has the form 'For all x, if x is unpunctual, x is reprehensible' (Ramsey [1965], 114). The more common example in the current literature is to propose 'Everything which is red is colored' as an analysis of 'Red is a color'. Russell's actual example, however, is of paraphrasing " 'Before' is a relation' as 'If I say that x is before y, I assert a relation between x and y" ([PLA], 182). The example is meant primarily to illustrate the essentially predicative nature of qualities, that 'before' must relate individuals. It is not presented as an example of a reduction of a higher order sentence to one of the first order. As well, Russell's example ascribes a formal property to 'before', one that might well have a complete analysis in logical terms, unlike the more factual 'Red is a color'. Ramsey is criticizing Russell for not fully realising the real consequences of his new commitment to extensionalism.[20] One such consequence was failing to see that he would also have to abandon higher order qualities. Russell seems to have only half understood this claim.

While Ramsey says that Russell should deny the existence of second order qualities, we in fact find many passages to the contrary in the logical atomism papers. For example, Russell considers the role of 'exists' in 'Colours exist in the spectrum between blue and yellow' ([PLA], 225). One would expect here some paraphrase in terms of *objects*, along the lines of 'red *things* are colored'. Instead he says of the original, "That would be a perfectly respectable statement, the colours being taken as universals. You mean simply that the propositional function 'x is a colour between blue and yellow' is one which is capable of truth. But the x

---

[20]See Russell's ([1931] and [1932]) reviews of Ramsey, where Russell seems to take Ramsey as so criticizing him.

which occurs there is not a particular, it is a universal" ([PLA], 225). This passage appears in a paragraph in which Russell discusses what it means to say that a particular exists. It certainly does not mean, he says, that the particular is not a universal, for asserting *that*, he says, would involve a type violation. "When I say of a universal that it exists, I should be meaning it in a different sense from that in which one says that particulars exist." That, I take it, is because particulars and universals belong to different types. Statements about the existence of a colour between blue and yellow are both existential generalisations over universals and of a different type from other existence claims.

In a letter to Wittgenstein from 1924, Ramsey complains that Russell did not understand much of Wittgenstein's views, and that all Russell did make of them was the view that "it is nonsense to put an adjective where a substantive ought to be, which helps with his theory of types".[21] Russell does seem to have come to view universals as of different types, or at least as fundamentally predicative. He does not seem to have come to the view that a proper, extensional theory of logic would have to be only second order as a consequence.[22]

There are some statements in PM, however, which do seem to commit Russell to the view that particulars and universals are of the same logical type. Nicholas Griffin has examined this evidence as part of a larger project of identifying the defects that Wittgenstein found in the multiple relation theory of judgment ([1980], 173). As he points out, this view is not in keeping with many things that Russell says about universals and types in other works. Such uncertainty might encourage an interpretation such as Cocchiarella's, which considers Russell to be in the process of changing his ontology from propositional functions to universals. Griffin holds that in the PM version of the multiple relation theory, universals must be of the same type as particulars. His argument is that they must both be classified logically as *individuals*. 'Individual' is the term that Russell uses for entities of the lowest logical type. The variables 'a', 'b','c','x','y','z', . . . range over them. Russell says of individuals: 'Such objects will be constituents of propositions or functions, and will be genuine constituents, in the sense that they do not disappear on analysis" ([PM], 51). The symbols for first order matrices are ϕx, $\psi(x,y)$, etc. , where "the arguments, however many there may be, are all individuals" ([PM], 51). As an explication of the notion he gives, in fact, a second characterization:

---

[21] Cited above from Monk ([1990], 219). At PLA (182) Russell begins his discussion of the universals and types with a similar acknowledgement to Wittgenstein.

[22] Cocchiarella argues that it is a consequence which Russell did not recognize. That is compatible with his still firm belief, at the time of Logical Atomism, that the logic is not extensional, and that there is a whole hierarchy of types of predicates.

Primitive Idea: Individual. We say that x is an 'individual'
if x is neither a proposition nor a function. ([PM], 132)

Griffin points out that since universals are constituents of propositions
that do not disappear upon analysis, they are individuals by the first
test. Secondly, they are neither propositions nor functions, so they are
individuals by the second test as well.

This conclusion can be avoided. In the first "definition", at PM (51),
Russell only says that these objects *are* genuine constituents of propositions, not that they are all the constituents, the *only* constituents. It
may well be that the symbols 'ϕ' and 'ψ' represent constituents of propositions that are *not* individuals. The second definition in fact makes a
distinction between entities referred to by the symbols of the language
of PM. In fact there is no 'symbol in isolation', no term, that denotes
a universal on its own, so this definition is simply distinguishing the
well-formed expressions such as '$\phi\hat{x}$', 'p', and 'a'. The first represents
a propositional function, the second a proposition, and the third, an
individual. Universals just do not appear here.

In *Principia* symbols for universals would be 'incomplete symbols', ie.
symbols with no independent meaning, for which, however, there is no
contextual definition possible. In "Logical Atomism" Russell says:

> Attributes and relations, though they may be not suscepti-
> ble of analysis, differ from substances by the fact that they
> suggest a structure, and that there can be no significant sym-
> bol which symbolises them in isolation. All propositions in
> which an attribute or a relation *seems* to be the subject are
> only significant if they can be brought into a form in which
> an attribute is attributed or a relation relates. If this were
> not the case, there would be significant propositions in which
> an attribute or a relation would occupy a position appropri-
> ate to a substance, which would be contrary to the doctrine
> of types, and would produce contradictions. Thus the proper
> symbol for 'yellow' (assuming for the sake of illustration that
> this is an attribute) is not the single word 'yellow', but the
> propositional function '$\hat{x}$ is yellow', where the structure of
> the symbol shows the position which the word 'yellow' must
> have if it is to be significant. ([LA], 174)

(Notice that while it is debatable whether 'yellow' is an attribute there
could be no question about the existence of the propositional function
'$\hat{x}$ is yellow'.) Thus within the logically accurate symbolism of PM there
will be no well-formed term standing alone for a universal, and so a
contrast only with propositional functions and propositions can identify

individuals adequately. Frege held that concepts are "unsaturated" and hence cannot be named. Russell has circumflex terms for propositional functions, and for him it is rather universals that cannot be named.[23] Universals can be seen in the symbolism of PM, however. The proposition 'Socrates is mortal' would be symbolized as 'ϕa' where 'a' is a name (or more likely definite description since Socrates is only known to us by description), and 'ϕ' symbolizes 'mortality'. That proposition does not have as a constituent the propositional function '$\hat{x}$ is mortal' symbolized by '$\phi\hat{x}$'; rather it is the universal *mortality* which is a constituent. (Remember that understanding the proposition does not require viewing it as a value of that propositional function, and only 'ϕ' and whatever else is required for the understanding is a constituent.)

This account of the symbols which stand for universals is explicit in the introduction to the second edition of PM. There, after listing the forms of atomic propositions as '$R_1, R_2(x, y), R_3(x, y, z), \ldots$' and saying that the x's can appear in different forms with different numbers of argument places or adicities, but the R's cannot, he offers this definition:

> Terms which can occur in any form of atomic proposition are called 'individuals' or 'particulars'; terms which occur as the R's occur are called 'universals'. ([PM], xix)

Universals are designated by the predicates of atomic sentences, 'R', rather than by the symbols for propositional functions, '$R\hat{x}$'.

It is clear that in his 1925 paper "Universals" ([1965], 112–134) Ramsey is *criticizing* a view he attributes to Russell, namely that universals and particulars differ in type. So at least Ramsey thought that Russell held this view. Ramsey refers to Russell's earlier papers on universals, from the time of PM, and not only to the later Logical Atomism lectures. Ramsey argues both that Russell's location of universals in parts of expressions for propositional functions is a mistaken consequence of the subjective interest of mathematicians in functions, and that Russell should have followed his commitment to extensionalism further to its natural consequence that there are no higher order entities. Ramsey joins W.E. Johnson in criticising Russell's analysis of atomic propositions into a subject term 's' and a propositional function '$\hat{x}$ is p'. Johnson advocated the traditional subject-copula-predicate analysis of 's is p'. Ramsey claimed to be following Wittgenstein in denying both John-

---

[23] As would be expected, Cocchiarella explains this as a change of view about whether universals/propositional functions can be named, under the influence of Wittgenstein. He sees Russell as continuously struggling with the Fregean problem of whether predicative entities can be named, whether those predicative entities are universals or propositional functions at different times.

son's predicative tie, represented by the copula, and what Ramsey represents as Russell's claim that "copulation is performed by universals" ([1965], 129). Ramsey himself wanted to follow Wittgenstein's theory that "the objects hang on one another like the links of a chain" ([1965], 129) and so will all be of one logical type. The distinction of subject and predicate, Ramsey says, comes from the analysis of universal generalization by which atomic facts are collected in different ways. We have, he says, no knowledge of the real nature of atomic facts; in particular, we do not know their analysis into particulars and universals. (Now here Ramsey is clearly identifying the view that a proposition can be analyzed into individuals and propositional functions in different ways with the view that it can be analyzed into particulars and universals in different ways. Ramsey missed the distinction between universals and propositional functions, as have the commentators who see Russell as switching his ontology from realist universals to nominalist predicates.)

As with propositional functions, the claim that universals are represented by *incomplete* symbols leads to difficulties. There is clearly no way in which the occurrence of universals in atomic propositional functions $F\hat{x}$ could be eliminated by some contextual analysis. So Russell allows the occurrence of an unanalyzable incomplete symbol, unlike the class symbols and definite descriptions, for which there is such an analysis. Not all incomplete symbols will be eliminable with contextual definitions. There are other difficulties as well. If, as I have suggested, Russell might countenance higher order universals, as in 'There are colours between blue and yellow', how would he analyze such second order predication? Consider 'Yellow is a colour'. If 'yellow' expresses a universal and must show its predicative nature, the whole expression will have to have as a constituent the propositional function '$\hat{x}$ is yellow'. A logical property like 'being a property' or 'being exemplified' can be expressed using first order quantifiers, '$\hat{\phi}\exists x\phi x$', as Russell's example of 'being a relation' shows. But what about the second order property of being a colour? How can an expression containing the propositional function '$\hat{x}$ is yellow' be about the *colour* rather than the propositional function? A distinction of constants into types would help, say by using 'Φ', 'Y' and 'a' respectively for second order universals, first order universals, and individuals, allowing both 'ΦY' and 'Ya' to be well formed. This distinction would observe Russell's thesis that the same term does not occur both as a subject and predicate, since the *type* of the symbol 'Y' shows its capacity to occur in predicates. But Russell does not have individual or predicate constants in PM, and the higher order variables all range over propositional *functions*, are all that is necessary for the mathematical purposes of PM.

Universals, I conclude, do figure in the metaphysics of PM, and are not to be identified with propositional functions. While universals should be distinguished by type, and so are not individuals, there is no free standing expression for them in PM. Symbols for universals can only occur in symbols for propositional functions from which the universals are twice removed by "construction". Thus while Russell did consider the ontological underpinnings of his logic when writing the introduction of *Principia Mathematica*, he did not work them out in detail. With only a tacit grasp of the difference between propositional functions and universals, he did not work out how PM could be a "logic" of universals.

3

PROPOSITIONS

The notion of a "Russellian Proposition" has recently come into common use in philosophical logic from the theory of "direct reference". In this chapter I want to discuss what Russell himself thought of these propositions. In what sense were his propositions "Russellian"? Why did he abandon propositions around 1910 and instead adopt his notorious "multiple relation" theory of belief, which, I claim, was the metaphysics of propositions in PM?

The term "Russellian Propositions" was introduced into recent discussions of propositional attitudes by David Kaplan as a way of explaining his notion of "direct reference". Kaplan distinguishes between what he calls "contexts of use" and "circumstances of evaluation". Contexts of use are familiar as the occasions for speech acts, and are essential for interpreting indexical expressions like 'I' or 'now'. An utterance and a context of use deliver a content, which is then evaluated with respect to a circumstance of evaluation to determine a truth value. Possible worlds and times are the most prominent examples of circumstances of evaluation.

> If I may wax metaphysical in order to fix an image, let us think of the vehicles of evaluation – the what-is-said in a given context – as a proposition. Don't think of the propositions as sets of possible worlds, but rather as structured entities looking something like the sentences which express them. For each occurence of a singular term in a sentence there will be a corresponding constituent in the proposition expressed. The constituent of the proposition determines, for each circumstance of evaluation, the object relevant to evaluating the proposition in that circumstance. In general, the constituent of the proposition will be some sort of complex, constructed from various attributes by logical composition. But in the case of a singular term which is directly refer-

ential, the constituent of the proposition is just the object itself. ([1989], 496)

Kaplan attributes this "metaphysical picture" of a proposition's structure to "the semantical parts of Russell's *Principles of Mathematics*". He goes on to say that Russell abandoned this picture by 1905 with "On Denoting", where he argued that definite descriptions do not stand for constituents of propositions at all, but rather are to be analysed via the contextual definitions of the theory of descriptions. What Russell abandoned in 1905 was a certain account of definite descriptions and names, namely the view that both contribute constituents to propositions. On this earlier view, names contribute an object and descriptions contribute a denoting concept. However, Russell did not give up until much later the central part of his account of propositions: that they are structured entities including objects and attributes. What I want to characterize as the doctrine of "Russellian" propositions, then, is the essential and surviving portion of the doctrine that interests Kaplan, the view that propositions are structured entities, having as constituents the regular individuals that they are "about". Russell kept this part of his view of propositions past 1905 and on to at least 1908. What he changed in 1905 was a view about what the particular constituents of propositions might be, and what elements of the surface form of sentences would introduce those entities into propositions. The central part of the surviving doctrine is that propositions are complex structured entities having objects as constituents. Indeed, Russell maintained a semantic correlate of this doctrine for quite a while. As late as 1912, after he had abandoned propositions, he still insisted that "Every proposition which we can understand must be composed wholly of constituents with which we are acquainted" ([PoP], 58).

This assertion, which has come to be known as "Russell's Principle" in the work of Gareth Evans and his followers, deserves some comment ([1982], 65 and chapter 4). It is certainly odd for someone who doesn't believe in propositions to say that all of them must nevertheless have constituents of a certain sort. Gareth Evans, Stephen Neale and others have stressed the notion of *understanding* in Russell's principle, and see the principle as a thesis about understanding language. The idea behind Evans' version of Russell is that talk of objects as constituents or somehow as existing *in* propositions can be replaced by talk of "object dependent" propositions. This is explained in terms of the epistemological notions of understanding and knowing what something is. A sentence expresses an object dependent proposition if one must know what object the singular term refers to in order to understand the proposition expressed. If there is no referent then there is no proposition; that is, no proposition is expressed or understood. As developed by Stephen Neale, for instance, this conception supposedly captures all that is needed for the theory of direct reference. He charges that no notion of objects as *constituents* of propositions is needed at all to explain the theory of proper names and the objections to the Fregean theory of sense (Neale [1990], chapter 2.2).

Kaplan describes his own notion as an "image" that results from "waxing metaphysical". How literally should we take the talk of objects as *constituents* of Russellian propositions? The theory of "direct reference" is a rival to the Fregean theory of *sense*. Names, and other directly referential devices, are held to designate their referents *without* the mediation of any sense, not via any properties that could be encapsulated in a "route to the referent". Most directly referential connections are established by a causal connection of some sort. For the purposes of defending the semantic theory of direct reference, then, it might be enough to say that one cannot place epistemological constraints on when certain propositions can be expressed, or sentences "understood". The metaphysical "picture" could remain just that, an image to help understand the two stages of semantic assessment, interpretation in a context and then evaluation. In other words, Kaplan might be able to define his notion of proposition in opposition to Evans. The essential feature of a Russellian proposition for Kaplan's semantics may well be indeed that one *doesn't* have to "know which" thing one is talking about to assert one. For the purposes of semantic theory it might be possible to leave the talk of constituents as just a suggestive image which reminds us that the object itself is important, not how we get at it cognitively.

Whatever the appropriateness of Evans' account of "Russell's Principle" for elucidating Kaplan's semantic proposals, my question is, rather, to what extent does the principle represent what Russell was up to? Do these epistemological notions of knowing what something is and understanding what was said capture the substance of *Russell's* propositions? Russell does speak of acquaintance as necessary for understanding propositions, and does even say that acquaintance requires "knowing what" you are talking about, but these are not epistemologically rich notions. As it is normally used by Russell, "acquaintance" does not require much recognition or ability to "reidentify". For one thing, the primary objects of acquaintance are sense data, which are not repeated, and thus are never around again to be reidentified. Secondly, acquaintance doesn't seem to require much categorization, as does an epistemologically loaded notion like "knowing who" someone is, in the sense of being able to distinguish them from others or to "individuate" them in some useful way. We can be acquainted with a patch of color, but not be certain what color predicate, such as 'red', applies to it. Terms such as 'red' are vague and require definition. Indeed Russell says that the judgment that a patch is red is really of the form 'there is that' ([PoP], 114) (where the 'that' seems to identify a color universal ostensively, and not in a way that presents its relations to other colors). Acquaintance gives us knowledge *of* an object, not necessarily any knowledge *about* it. Thus:

> The particular shade of colour that I am seeing may have many things said about it – I may say that it is brown, that it is rather dark, and so on. But such statements, though they make me know truths *about* the colour, do not make me know the colour itself any better than I did before: so far as concerns knowledge of the colour itself, as opposed to knowledge of truths about it, I know the colour perfectly and completely when I see it, and no further knowledge of it is even theoretically possible. ([PoP], 47)

This suggests that the knowledge that a sense datum is brown may not be certain, or at least is not knowledge directly delivered by acquaintance. Acquaintance with sense data does not provide us with an incorrigible foundation for epistemology, as might be thought. Evans considers as a form of acquaintance our ability to recognize faces, which does not require categorization or any explicit sort of "knowing who" someone is. Still, even that sort of minimal epistemological content is not essential to acquaintance for Russell. His concern was with the logical form of things in the world, in particular the structural properties of the facts that make up beliefs. Thus he considers whether or not belief is a relation between a self and a propositional object. If so, the objects to which we are related would have to exist, and that possibility he rejects in the case of false propositions. The feature of relations such as acquaintance and understanding that most concerned Russell was that they required existing relata. Even after rejecting the existence of propositions as independent entities, propositions treated just as meaningful sentences still involved a series of existing objects of acquaintance for their interpretation.

But surely we can *understand* sentences with non-denoting names? I think that Russell used the notion of understanding in a very thin way as well. Understanding a proposition is analogous to acquaintance with an object. It is propositions that he spoke of understanding, not sentences or utterances. A better expression for this would be "entertaining", a term for that minimal relation to a proposition that must be attained before it can be the object of a more specific attitude, such as belief. Now it may be that on occasion Russell made the notions of acquaintance and understanding bear a bit more of their ordinary epistemological load than I have suggested. Such epistemological notions, however, do not outweigh the metaphysical content of the theory.

3.1 RUSSELL ABANDONS PROPOSITIONS

For Russell, it was important that propositions were complex entities with objects somehow as constituents. This is the core of the long running theory of propositions that Russell abandoned with his "multiple relation" theory of belief, which in turn came to span at least the period from 1908 to 1918. The basic idea of the new theory was that belief does not relate an individual to a proposition composed of various individuals and universals, but rather relates the believer directly to those constituents. In his example, Othello's belief that Desdemona loves Cassio relates Othello, Desdemona, Cassio and the relation of loving, rather than Othello and the proposition that Desdemona loves Cassio.

There has been much discussion of Russell's later abandonment of this doctrine, in particular of the influence of Wittgenstein's criticism of it.[1] Here I discuss instead Russell's reasons for *adopting* the doctrine in the first place, and thus for abandoning the earlier "Russellian Propositions".

Russell's reasons for abandoning propositions may at first seem rather weak. I want to argue that they are in fact rather compelling. Let us take Russell's arguments in the *Philosophy of Logical Atomism* as a starting point. Lecture IV is devoted to belief. First a statement of Russell's project:

> I think that one might describe philosophical logic, the portion of logic which is the portion that I am concerned with in these lectures since Christmas, as an inventory, or if you like a more humble word, a "Zoo" containing all the different forms that facts may have. I should prefer to say "forms of facts" rather than "forms of propositions" ... In accordance with the sort of realistic bias that I should put into all study of metaphysics, I should always wish to be engaged in the investigation of some actual fact or set of facts, and it seems to me that this is so in logic just as it is in zoology. In logic you are concerned with the forms of facts, with getting hold of the different forms of facts, different *logical* sorts of facts, that there are in the world. ([PLA], 191)

---

[1] See Nicholas Griffin [1980]. Russell was still presenting the theory, though tentatively, in PLA in 1918, long after he was supposedly shattered by Wittgenstein's criticisms in 1913.

To our ears this passage is an indication of a confusion of logic and metaphysics and of logical analysis with metaphysical analysis. I will try to show below, however, that as with Kaplan, certain logical views suggest a certain metaphysical "picture" of propositions, and that the combination of Russell's metaphysical views and accompanying logical views makes good sense of his abandonment of propositions.

The abandonment of propositions follows from denying that belief sentences such as "I believe that Socrates is mortal" have the form "I believe the proposition p". The objection Russell gives is that such an analysis cannot account for false beliefs: "It is obvious from the fact that you can believe a false belief that you cannot cut off one part: you cannot have I believe/Socrates is mortal" ([PLA], 192). Why is this obvious?

Russell asserts that it is his commitment to realism that leads him to abandon his belief in propositions.

> Time was when I thought there were propositions, but it does not seem to me very plausible to say that in addition to facts there are also these curious shadowy things going about such as "That today is Wednesday" when it is in fact Tuesday. I cannot believe they go about the real world. It is more than one can manage to believe, and I do not think a person with a vivid sense of reality can imagine it. ([PLA], 196)

> When I speak of the proposition "That today is Wednesday" I do not mean the occurrence in future of a state of mind in which you think it is Wednesday, but I am thinking about the theory that there is something quite logical, something not involving the mind in any way; and such a thing as that I do not think you can take a false proposition to be. ([PLA], 197)

Is this argument anything more than what David Lewis ([1986], §2.8) calls "the incredulous stare", the blank incomprehension which he himself encounters when defending possible worlds? Surely, we might think, Russell has confused propositions as *truth bearers* with facts which are *truth makers*, that he has confused metaphysics, which for a realist is the study of a reality independent of minds, with logic, which for a (platonist) realist like Russell, has room for abstract entities such as propositions. Surely, one would say, Russell's objections to Meinong's theory of objects should not extend to all logical objects, in particular to Frege's theory of thoughts (*Gedanke*) which serve as meanings? Russell believed in universals, so why not other abstract entities as well, other denizens of the "third realm" which might only "subsist"? To attribute to Russell a dislike of propositions on ontological grounds alone makes him out to be a nominalist in a way quite incompatible with his realism about other things, such as universals.

3.2   THE UNITY OF PROPOSITIONS

What can one say in Russell's defense? Russell wanted to do away with logical entities over and above the facts, universals and particulars that he already acknowledged. He identified true propositions with facts, for it seemed that the objects of knowledge and perception are things standing in relation to others, facts. False propositions, then, like the proposition that "Today is Wednesday" uttered on Tuesday, would have to be *false* or *non-existent* facts. What did he find objectionable about false facts? I believe it was what they would have in common with true propositions, if such propositions were to be distinguished from facts. It is really his objections to propositions, as distinct from facts, that we must look at. Russell did want to get rid of what *we* might think of as distinctively logical entities, such as Fregean Thoughts. The problem before us is to explain why he would do this, while still being a realist about universals and other abstract entities.

Why did Russell avoid propositions, whether true or false? The problem is not with their constituents, the objects and universals with which they are composed, but rather in their combination, the unity that holds them together.[2] Kenneth Olson [1987] maintains that Russell had thought that Bradley's regress argument was directed against the existence of relations, when they were actually arguments for facts. The problem was that a's being related by R to b cannot simply be the plurality of a, R and b, since something has to hold them together. This cohesion cannot be accomplished just by another relation R' because then something would have to hold R' together with R, a and b, and so on. According to Olson, Bradley held that it was the *fact* of a's bearing R to b that held them together. And indeed, it did so for Russell. Olson's suggestion, then, is that Russell himself acknowledged facts for the very reasons given by Bradley, but without realizing the source of the reasoning.

Whatever the origin of Russell's view about facts, the following seems to be the role facts played in his reasoning. Any sort of "unity" involving a, R, and b could only consist of a's bearing R to b, namely, *a fact*

---

[2]Here I follow Olson ([1987], 80) "... a relation either relates a pair of terms or it does not. This made it rather hard for Russell to account for the unity of a false proposition, since it could not consist in the fact that the relation which is asserted to hold actually holds. And this put pressure on him to deny propositions in favor of facts." This is the thesis which I wish to defend in this chapter.

that requires that a bear R to b.[3] What if a does not bear R to b? In PLA, Russell repeats his tentative endorsement of negative facts, facts that would be "falsity makers" for false atomic sentences. A negative fact would make 'Socrates is alive' false, and thus 'Socrates is not alive' true. In general, when *not aRb* is true there will be some fact to that effect, *a's not bearing R to b*. That worried Russell, but was not nearly so difficult for him as accepting *false* facts. Negative facts would only require a distinctive mode of combination of objects and universals, a new variety of predication, which would tie objects together in a negative way. What a false fact would require, however, is two dimensions to predication. A "false fact", that aRb, which would subsist or have being when a does not bear R to b and would presumably involve the existing entities a, b and R, yet still fail to obtain or exist. Only the way the existing objects are put together could make a "false" fact which does not exist or obtain. I think it was accepting such a special form of combination that was too much for Russell. The only mode of combination that he could see was predication, although he considered the idea that there might be two sorts of predication, having and failing to have a property. We might think that the negative form of predication in negative facts could be made to account for the "unity" of the false fact as well. However, a false atomic fact couldn't be the same as a negative fact, for then a's bearing R to b, the false fact, would be the same as a's *not* bearing R to b, the negative fact. But those can't be the same thing.[4] With true propositions Russell's difficulty is even clearer. A true proposition, distinct from the fact it reports, would have to bind the individuals together to form a unity, but not a unity that made for a fact. One would need something to hold a, R and b together, and then something else about the way they are held together that would make the proposition that aRb true.

In summary, then, I propose that we read Russell's remark that he cannot believe in such "curious shadowy things going about as 'That today is Wednesday' when in fact it is Tuesday" as follows. If it is true that today is Tuesday then there is such a fact as today's being Tuesday. There may also be a *negative* fact, viz. today's *not* being Wednesday, which contains today and being Wednesday in a special negative fash-

---

[3] It is the search for some other way of uniting the entities that leads to the multiple relation theory. Thus, "Suppose we wish to understand "A and B are similar". It is essential that our thought should, as is said, "unite" or "synthesize" the two terms and the relation; but we cannot *actually* "unite" them, since either A and B are similar, in which case they are already united, or they are dissimilar, in which case no amount of thinking can force them to become united" ([ToK], 116). (See also 80 and 98 for talk of relations "as relating" and for the unity of propositions.)

[4] This argument was suggested to me by David Braun.

ion. But there is not *also* a proposition of today's being Wednesday, a complex combining today and being Wednesday in a way that does not produce the *fact* of today's being Wednesday; for there is no such fact. Indeed there is no way that objects combine except to form positive (or perhaps also negative) facts. There are no propositions because there is nothing to hold them together, nothing to make objects "constituents" of propositions.

To say that Russell acknowledged no compound entities other than facts is to attribute a fairly strongly atomistic metaphysics to him, one more familiar from Wittgentstein's *Tractatus* than Russell's atomism. We do, however, find Russell explicitly endorsing this view in his 1919 paper "On Propositions: What They Are and How They Mean" ([CP8], 278–306). He says "I mean by a 'fact' anything that is complex. If the world contains no simples, then whatever it contains is a fact …". He immediately makes clear that this applies to individuals as well with the parenthetical remark that "For the purposes of illustration, I am for the moment neglecting the fact that Socrates and Plato are themselves complex". A footnote to the section on facts asserts that it does not contain new material, but rather views that have been defended "elsewhere" ([CP8], 278). Just how far back does the view go? Quite a bit, I think. The view that everything real must be either a simple or a fact was part of Russell's views from before the multiple relation theory of judgment and must be compatible with the views expressed in PM.[5] This is not the fully developed atomism clearly influenced by Wittgenstein which shows up in the PLA lectures. In this early version, it is only *objects* that must be simple. Facts, however, are not limited to the simple, atomic facts, they can be negative and general and perhaps complex in other ways.

3.3   COMPLEX ENTITIES

Russell begins his exposition of the multiple relation theory in PM as follows:

> The universe consists of objects having various qualities and standing in various relations. Some of the objects which occur in the universe are complex. When an object is complex, it consists of interrelated parts. Let us consider a complex object composed of two parts a and b standing to each other in the relation R. The complex object "a-in-the-relation-R-to-b" may be capable of being *perceived*; when perceived, it

---

[5] Hylton [1990] presents a similar account of Russell's rejection of propositions and his fact based metaphysics. He is less sanguine about the chances of making the logic of PM out as compatible with these metaphysical views.

is perceived as one object. Attention may show that it is
complex; we then *judge* that *a* and *b* stand in the relation *R*.
([PM], 43)

This passage expresses Russell's distinctive view that in perception
we are directly acquainted with facts. Direct perception must be veridi-
cal, we perceive *facts*. But it is also clear that this passage suggests that
"complex objects", things with interrelated parts, just are *facts*. This
passage, and the whole section on the multiple relation theory, might be
seen as signs of a change of mind, a development out of keeping with
the rest of PM. I want to argue that it is not. My claim may seem false,
for, after all, didn't Russell acknowledge (and even quantify over) propositional functions, which could have any complexity, corresponding, as
they do, to every open sentence which is consistent with type theory?
Presumably for every sentence, no matter how complex, one could produce an open sentence, and thus require the existence of a propositional
function, merely by deleting a single name and replacing it with a variable? In §2 it was claimed that he did not. Russell did not believe that
propositional functions were genuine complex entities. Russell was committed to taking them every bit as much as "logical constructions" as
propositions.

That propositions and propositional functions were both constructions does not mean that Russell had no room for peculiarly logical entities. When he describes those things with which we can be acquainted,
and which are therefore genuine entities, he includes "... relations of
space and time, similarity and certain abstract logical universals" ([PoP],
109). In the *Theory of Knowledge* manuscript there is more time devoted
to logical universals. It was complex entities that he rejected.

This rejection returns us then to the argument against the existence of
propositions, be they true or false. The only mode of combination of *a*, *R*
and *b* which can obtain is the actual relating of *a* and *b* by *R*, which only
exists if the fact that *aRb* exists. (Or perhaps also the combination that
results when the fact that *not aRb* obtains, if there are negative facts.)
There are no true propositions to contrast with facts. Russell could as
easily have argued that he couldn't really understand how, when it is
Tuesday, there could be the the proposition that today is Tuesday in
addition to the fact that today is Tuesday. That duplication would be
just as questionable. What bothered him was the mere existence of the
representational complex in addition to the facts that are represented.

Why was Russell reluctant to postulate other forms of complexity
in objects? To us it seems so easy to postulate complex objects, even
simple mereological sums or, more often, sets of objects. This is indeed

the standard representation of Russellian propositions as used in formal semantics. A singular or Russellian proposition is modeled as an n-tuple consisting of a relation (propositional function) and $n - 1$ individuals. Notice, however, that this is just a *model* of propositions and that a good case can be made for demanding more of a theory of propositions and an account of precisely what constituency in a proposition amounts to. One cannot simply identify propositions with sets without prejudging certain questions about them. For example, if constituents are simply members of propositions, then if sets are wellfounded, no proposition can be a member of itself, and so no proposition can be directly about itself.[6] Is that obviously the case? It might well be, but only because the "constituent of" relations between objects and propositions are wellfounded, not because sets are wellfounded. In any case, we should examine impartially the metaphysics of propositions without importing all of the features of sequences into the theory of propositions. If one is going to be realist about propositions, one ought to allow them their own metaphysics and principles of construction.

Russell's view, as a logicist, was that sets are rather to be analyzed in terms of propositional functions, and so sets are logical constructions. But there is also a reason for an atomist not to analyze functions as complex sets. A thoroughgoing atomist wants to reduce complex objects in terms of *logical* relations between simple objects, and, when the atomism is based on facts, in terms of logically complex facts involving simple objects. It was this project which sounds so very odd to us when it was later criticised by Wittgenstein.[7] It sounds bizarre to ask about the *logically simple* parts of a broom. Are they the handle and brush, or something else? We sense that obviously logical and physical analysis are being confused. We talk about objects as sums of physical atoms, not logical atoms. But a genuine logical atomist, it seems, really does want to analyse complex individuals as *logical compounds* of their parts! We see the mereological sum of two individuals as simply another individual related to the former by the part of relation. Russell, however, must have seen even wholes as somehow *logically* related to their parts, as logical constructions from those parts.

Chapter XVI, "Whole and Part", of *Principles of Mathematics* is devoted to a discussion of the part/whole relationship. There Russell distinguishes two kinds of wholes, "unities" and "aggregates". Aggregates are given completely when their parts are given. They are also of the same logical type as their parts. Unities require some structure

---

[6] See Barwise and Etchemendy [1987] for this view of propositions, as well as the use of "non-wellfounded" sets to model self-referential propositions.

[7] At *Philosophical Investigations*, §60.

as well. Thus the proposition "A differs from B" requires not only the constituents A, B and difference, but also a structure or logical form. Russell still considers the relation of a part to the whole in a formless aggregate to be a *logical* relation, one that must be taken as a primitive logical relation along with the relation of a member to a class, and one which thus cannot be defined in terms of other such relations. I think that even contemporary philosophers, with our grasp of mereology, must admit that the '*part of*' relation is close to 'ϵ' (set membership) on the continuum of logical to non-logical terms. Russell only acknowledged classes as fictional unities constructed from a plurality. This general view includes not seeing propositions as sets of objects and properties, but as somehow logically analyzed in terms of them.[8] How would the analysis of complex objects proceed? To use Wittgenstein's example, a "complex" object such as a broom will be reducible to a fact involving simple objects, say, that the brush is attached to the handle. To say that the brush is a *part* of the broom is to say that there is some fact of the form: this brush is attached to this handle, and the brush is a constituent of that fact. Thus the part/whole relationship will ultimately be reduced to talk of objects as constituents of facts. Talk of complex objects will be reduced to talk of facts and their constituents. This reduction seems to be what Russell had in mind.

My interpretation attempts to reconcile several seemingly incompatible aspects of Russell's thought. It may be that his thought was in flux and that reconciliation is just not possible. Certainly Russell did not provide the sort of analysis and contextual definitions of propositions that he did for the reduction of classes to propositional functions. It is hard to imagine what such an analysis would look like.[9] Still, however, it seems possible to understand how Russell could himself see his multiple relation theory as compatible with the logic of PM. It is not necessary to see the theory as a flatly inconsistent interpolation.

---

[8]In his introduction to *The Philosophy of Logical Atomism*, David Pears [1985] gives the name "structural essentialism" to Russell's views about the relation of an object and its parts. He argues that for Russell the name of any object with parts will be analyzable in terms of names for its ultimate parts. That structural analysis is essential to the object and is to be contrasted with descriptions which only pick it out contingently.

[9]Leonard Linsky has pointed out to me that while Russell seems to want to avoid quantifying over propositions in his discussion of *14·3 of PM, "In this proposition, however, the use of propositions as apparent variables involves an apparatus not required elsewhere, and we have therefore not used this proposition in subsequent proofs". Not "required" rather than not *allowed* because it would commit him to propositions? I suspect that Russell could hold that propositions were really nothing while still allowing some quantification over them.

Modern analysis allows itself two sorts of combination with which to "construct" entities: the unity of sets and mereological summation. For a logicist it would be possible to insist that set membership is a logical relation. But what about the relation of an object to a mereological sum, the part-whole relation? It would seem that a first order relation with a uniform field is not a logical relation. After all, parts and wholes are both simply objects, one does not even have the heterogeneity of sets and members. This is what made Nelson Goodman see mereology as the appropriate theory of objects for a nominalist. There are no peculiar logical objects in such a theory, it would seem.

But let us look at mereology more closely. What happens when we speak of time and change? Consider the notorious philosophical question: Is a bundle of sticks the same bundle when you take out one stick?[10] This problem may seem easily solved if one adopts an ontology of temporal stages and views ordinary objects as sums of their temporal parts. But now what if one worries about changes that have not actually occurred with bundles, but *might have*? Wouldn't the bundle (or the ship of Theseus) have been the very same thing if it had lost or gained some small piece? Now intuitions of mereological essentialism come to the fore, because sums have parts as essentially as sets have members, or so some think. But then one cannot identify ordinary persisting physical objects with the mereological sum of their parts, as materialists might want to. If one wants to identify the continuing bundle with its constituent sticks and allows sums to change parts across worlds, then having particular parts can't be an essential property of a sum. Mereological sums look more and more like substances.[11] A mereological sum is now something that can bind together disparate parts and cannot be seen as simply some object of exactly the same kind or type as those parts. Sums look more and more like the sort of things that raise questions of the one and the many, questions that Russell hoped to solve with logic.

I have argued that Russell's objections to propositions were a consequence of his atomism. For Russell, all complexes except for facts were logical constructions of the real entities, the genuine objects of his metaphysics. Propositions were complex objects, including objects and universals as constituents. They would only be logical constructions, not "real". What I have portrayed here is a logicist version of metaphysics. A logicist in mathematics reduces mathematical truths and objects to logical truths and objects. This logicist metaphysics reduces complex ob-

---

[10] One wag once asserted that half of the profession of philosophy takes this question seriously. The other half of our community has the therapeutic goal of curing the first half of interest in that question.

[11] See Ali Kazmi [1990] for a discussion of sums and change over time.

jects to logical constructions of simple objects. Russell's robust sense of logic would allow him to think that logic could bear some metaphysical weight.[12]

---

[12]Should a moral be drawn here for contemporary discussions of "Russellian Propositions"? The realism required to accept propositions will not be a problem. There is a well recognized need for abstract entities in semantics. The *unity* of propositions should be given more attention, however. There is a unity to a proposition, a connection between objects and universals which is not the same as the inherence tie, or whatever it is that relates objects and universals in facts. Now one can follow Russell's own strategy and try to *construct* propositions out of more familiar entities; in particular, as ordered sequences of objects and universals. But how are we to take these constructions? Are they really propositions, or do they just *model* them? Surely the latter. Are the objects of a proposition literally members of the proposition? Perhaps even some semantic issues can be resolved by an investigation of the metaphysics of propositions. How, for example, does a proposition have a truth value *at* each of many different possible worlds, including worlds in which its constituents don't exist? What is it to grasp a proposition? Do propositions have a unique structure or can they be "carved up" in different ways into constituents? Or perhaps it is even time to revive facts in our ontology, along with some of the other apparatus of logical atomism that was abandoned for whatever reasons there were that seemed so convincing at the time.

4

THE RAMIFIED THEORY OF TYPES

Russell's solution to the paradoxes was finally formulated in *Principia Mathematica* as "The Theory of Logical Types", or what has come to be known as the "Ramified" theory of types. It consists of a logical system which allows higher order quantifiers to range over propositional functions, as well as the famous theory of descriptions and the distinctive "No-classes" theory of classes. The logic had to have the power to allow the deduction of mathematics necessary to the logicist program, while simultaneously avoiding the paradoxes. This chapter will present a modern formulation of that theory, due primarily to Alonzo Church, and will show how some of the paradoxes are resolved and how this formulation differs only slightly from the system presented in PM. It will conclude with a brief look at rival formulations, arguing that the differences are not as great as one might think. While underdetermined and problematic by contemporary standards, there clearly is a unique and well motivated system of types in PM, one that can be assessed both as to the success of its solution to the paradoxes, and with regard to its metaphysical implications.

The next chapter will consider the justification that Russell provides for the theory of types with the vicious circle principle, and how several different things that Russell says about the structure of the hierarchy of types fit with that principle. I will urge that the preferred formulation is closest to the spirit of the theory and is in keeping with the justification of the vicious circle principle and the view of propositional functions as "constructions" that was defended above. It will then be possible in Chapter 6 to interpret the ontological significance of the axiom of reducibility.

4.1   CHURCH'S r-TYPES

Alonzo Church [1976] presents a formulation of the ramified theory of types which includes a type notation and some discussion of axioms. His type symbols indicate "r-types", defined as follows:

Individual variables belong to the r-type ι. If $\beta_1, \ldots, \beta_m$ are r-types and $m \geq 0$, then there is an r-type $(\beta_1, \ldots, \beta_m)/n$ of *level* n where $n \geq 1$.

The *order* of a variable is defined inductively.[1]

An individual variable is of order 0. The order of a variable of r-type $(\beta_1, \ldots, \beta_m)/n$ is $N + n$, where N is the greatest of the orders of $\beta_1, \ldots, \beta_m$ (and $N = 0$ if $m = 0$).

Variables of r-type $(\ )/n$ range over propositions of level n, variables of r-type $(\beta_1, \ldots, \beta_m)/n$, where $m > 0$, range over m-ary propositional functions of level n with arguments of types $\beta_1, \ldots, \beta_m$.

The r-type $(\alpha_1, \ldots, \alpha_m)/k$ is *directly lower* than $(\beta_1, \ldots, \beta_m)/n$ if $\alpha_1 = \beta_1, \ldots, \alpha_m = \beta_m$, and $k < n$.

The formation rules provide that propositional variables of type $(\ )/n$ are well-formed formulas (wffs). A formula $\phi(x_1, \ldots x_m)$ is well-formed if and only if ϕ is a variable or constant of the r-type $(\beta_1, \ldots, \beta_m)/n$, where $m > 0$, and x_1 is a variable or constant whose r-type is β_1 or directly lower than $\beta_1, \ldots$ and x_m is a variable or constant whose r-type is β_m or directly lower than β_m.[2]

Whenever ϕ and ψ are wffs and v is a variable, $\sim \phi$, $\phi \vee \psi$, and $(\forall v)\phi$ are wffs.[3]

This much corresponds to the syntax of a formal system. Formulating the rules of inference and axioms of PM is another task. While Russell notoriously does not distinguish rules of inference such as *modus ponens* from axioms, calling them all "primitive propositions", and does not make clear important syntactic distinctions such as the difference between schematic letters and free variables, these are all matters in which technical logic has advanced since 1910, and in which improvements would not amount to violations of the philosophical underpinnings of the theory.[4] Even with the later changes, the following (partial) list of primitive propositions in PM should look familiar to the contemporary logician.

The first proposition amounts to the rule of *modus ponens*, stated in

---

[1] If primitive constants are added they will have orders as well, but other terms and formulas are not assigned orders.

[2] The addition "or directly lower" makes the types cumulative, a seemingly minor departure from Russell's stricter notion of type.

[3] I will use the more recent notation '$(\forall v)$' for the universal quantifier instead of Russell's '(v)' to make formulas more easily readable, but will retain the original in quotations from PM.

[4] Jung [1994] has a careful discussion of these issues and presents a plausible "modernized" version of PM which resolves them.

∗1·1 for "elementary" or unquantified propositions only, and later in full generality as:

∗9·12 What is implied by a true premiss is true.

Taking '$\sim$' and '$\vee$' as primitive and defining '$\supset$' and conjunction in terms of them, the axioms for propositional logic are this list:

∗1·2 $\vdash : p \vee p. \supset .p$

∗1·3 $\vdash : q. \supset .p \vee q$

∗1·4 $\vdash : p \vee q. \supset .q \vee p$

∗1·5 $\vdash : p \vee (q \vee r). \supset .q \vee (p \vee r)$

(later shown to be redundant)

and

∗1·6 $\vdash : .q \supset r. \supset : p \vee q. \supset .p \vee r$

Russell intends that the rules and axioms that govern quantifiers should extend to all types. He attempts this with the device of "typical ambiguity", what could be captured in a modern system with the use of axiom schemas allowing all well-formed expressions of any type as instances. Church prefers to treat these axioms as formulas with variables, and to complete the system with rules of substitution.

The quantifier rules (following the development of ∗10 which takes the universal quantifier as primitive) are:

∗10·1 $\vdash : (x).\phi x. \supset \phi y$

∗10·11 If ϕy is true whatever possible argument y may be, then $(x).\phi x$ is true. In other words, whenever the propositional function ϕy can be asserted, so can the proposition $(x).\phi x$.

∗10·12 $\vdash : .(x).p \vee \phi x. \supset : p. \vee .(x)\phi x$

These three correspond exactly to familiar axioms for the universal quantifier and the rule of universal generalization, despite their unusual formulation.[5]

While a valuable exercise, the attempt to formulate a modern deductive system as close to the original of PM as possible is beyond the scope of this investigation. It is clear, however, that these seeming oddities of the original presentation do not undermine the system's philosophical coherence.

Church does not attempt to follow the axioms and inference rules of PM but instead presents his own formulation. It is based on his rules for the "Functional Calculus of Higher Order" (Church [1956], chapter 5)

---

[5]∗10·12 is the analogue to the more familiar axiom $(\forall x)(p \supset \phi x) \supset (p \supset (\forall x)\phi x)$. The rules for substituting expressions for variables are subject to the restrictions on type that hold for the comprehension principles below. See Church ([1976], 750).

with the addition of explicit comprehension schemas. Church ([1976] and [1984]) presents a different formulation. Church's [1976] rules include the following comprehension principle for propositional functions:[6]

$$(\exists f)(\forall x_1)(\forall x_2)\dots(\forall x_m)\,[f(x_1, x_2 \dots x_m) \equiv \phi]$$

where f is a functional variable of r-type $(\beta_1, \beta_2, \dots, \beta_m)/n$ and $x_1, x_2, \dots x_m$ are variables of r-types $\beta_1, \beta_2, \dots, \beta_m$ and the bound variables of ϕ are all of order less than the order of f, and the free variables of ϕ and the constants occurring in ϕ are all of order not greater than the order of f (and f does not occur free in ϕ).[7] Church also provides a principle for propositions:

$$(\exists p)\,[p \equiv \phi]$$

where p is a propositional variable of r-type $(\ )/n$, the bound variables of ϕ are all of order less than n, and the free variables and constants of ϕ are all of order not greater than n (and p does not occur free in ϕ). This principle is an addition to PM which, except for a few instances (including $*14\cdot3$), does not use bound, or "real", variables that range over propositions. Such quantification might seem incompatible with the apparent denial of the existence of propositions of the "multiple relation theory". The avoidance of bound propositional variables is rather just a result of the fact that propositions are not used in the development of mathematics, and not of some eliminativist ontological position.[8] Carrying out the logicist program of PM did not require the use of propositional variables in addition to the logic of propositional functions and thus of classes. Applications to other, intensional, phenomena such as some of the very paradoxes that motivate the theory of types does require quantifying over propositions, as will be seen below.

Because they use the material biconditional '$\equiv$', these comprehension principles only guarantee the existence of propositional functions coextensive with a given formula (or propositions truth functionally equivalent to a given sentence). For the extensional purposes of the construc-

---

[6] As corrected in Church [1984].

[7] Here I use 'ϕ' as a schematic letter, while elsewhere it is used as a variable.

[8] At PM (185) we find that "...$*14\cdot3$ introduces propositions (p, q namely) as apparent variables, which we have not done elsewhere, and cannot do legitimately without explicit introduction of the hierarchy of propositions with a reducibility-axiom such as $*14\cdot3$". This clearly indicates that propositional variables could be added if necessary alterations were made elsewhere including an additional version of the axiom of reducibility for propositions. This seems a matter of convenience rather than ontological principle. It will be argued below (in Chapter 7) that Russell's assertion that propositions are "incomplete symbols" is not incompatible with the use of quantifiers ranging over them. Indeed, it will be claimed that in this regard they do not differ from propositional functions.

tion of mathematics the existence of extensionally equivalent functions and propositions is adequate. For applications to logical theory, however, including the study of intensional contexts, stronger principles seem to be used. The existence of a particular proposition or function, not just of one equivalent to it, that must be asserted in certain derivations. Church ([1974] and [1984]) argues that PM does not allow anything but variables or constants to flank the '=' sign. Thus, for example, $p = (\exists x)(\forall y)[(Fy \equiv y = x) \wedge Gx]$ could not be expressed in PM, but would seem essential to an account of the very example involving definite descriptions and belief sentences, George IV and the author of *Waverly*, that Russell himself cites ([PM], 83–84) to illustrate the phenomena of intensionality with definite descriptions.

To rectify this shortcoming of PM, Church proposes the introduction of a new symbol ' $\equiv$ ' which can be flanked by formulas and variables.[9] A formula '$p \equiv \phi$' will be well-formed and is intended to express the identity of propositions. This intention is fulfilled by the addition of axioms for ' $\equiv$ ', asserting its connection with '='. For the purposes of what follows, however, I will express identity of propositions with '='. The reader who wants to follow Church may substitute ' $\equiv$ ' in the following wherever '=' flanks higher order variables.[10] Stronger comprehension principles can then be stated:

$$(\exists f)(\forall x_1)(\forall x_2)\ldots(\forall x_m)\,[f(x_1, x_2 \ldots x_m) = \phi]$$

and:

$$(\exists p)\,[p = \phi]$$

(subject to the same restrictions). The first says that for every $x_1 \ldots x_m$, the value of the propositional function f, relative to $x_1 \ldots x_m$, is the same as the proposition identified by ϕ (relative to $x_1 \ldots x_m$). The second asserts that p is the same proposition as ϕ. In what follows the principles using '=' will be needed to illustrate the resolution in PM of several paradoxes.

The analysis of the paradoxes and other issues in PM can proceed with the notions described so far, however, there are more features of

---

[9]This double use of sentences, so that they can occur in subject position as well as sententially, flanking sentence connectives, has seemed to border on incoherence to some. See Chihara ([1974], 27–28), who finds in this double use more evidence of use-mention confusions. The use of 'p' in sentential connectives is being confused, he says, with its mention in sentences apparently about the proposition. However, such double use of propositional variables would seem to be essential for any intensional logic allowing quantification over propositions, and is not special to the system of PM.

[10]See, however, C.A. Anderson [1989], who dissents from Church's strong axioms connecting ' $\equiv$ ' and '=', establishing a sharp distinction between the two.

the system that require discussion as well. One such is the use in PM of "circumflex" abstracts for propositional functions. The following, which looks like just another formation rule, in fact has the force of a comprehension principle since it generates terms which can then be existentially generalized:

> ∗9·15. If, for some a, there is a proposition ϕa, then there is a function $\phi \hat{x}$, and vice versa. Pp.

This axiom can be formulated as:[11]

$$(\forall y_1)(\forall y_2)\ldots(\forall y_n)[\phi \hat{x}_1 \ldots \hat{x}_n(y_1, \ldots y_n) \equiv \phi]$$

This one biconditional axiom captures both the "abstraction" principle for propositional functions, read right to left, and "conversion" for propositional abstracts, read left to right. In what follows it will be useful to consider abstracts as part of the system, as they appear to be in PM.

Russell says that he and Whitehead try to avoid use of circumflexed terms in PM: "In fact we have found it convenient and possible – except in the explanatory portions – to keep the explicit use of symbols of the type '$\phi \hat{x}$', either as constants [eg. $\hat{x} = a$] or as real variables, almost entirely out of this work." ([PM], 19). Landini ([1996], 305) interprets this to mean that circumflex expressions are a metalinguistic device for talking about open formulas, and that functions show up in the system only as the values of bound variables, never as referents of terms. (He goes on to insist that only predicative functions serve as values for higher order quantifiers, and thus no higher level functions appear at all in the ontology of PM.) Thus, he denies that circumflex expressions are term forming operators. I read this passage rather as a reflection of the fact that the symbolism of systems of abstracts, such as the λ-calculus, is subtle. The use of any variable binding operator leads to difficulties with scope. There must be some way to indicate the various orders in which the operator can be applied to bind different variables. The circumflex notation does appear in the body of PM, but is only given an incomplete analysis at ∗21.[12] The circumflex notation does, then, seem to be part of the system, but is not fully developed because it is really only essential to the introductory and philosophical aspects of the work. The proper use of circumflexes would have to be regimented with something like the notation of the λ-calculus to avoid these difficulties. Contrary to Landini, it seems that Whitehead and Russell may have been aware of

---

[11]Or

$$(\forall y_1)(\forall y_2)\ldots(\forall y_n)[\phi \hat{x}_1 \ldots \hat{x}_n(y_1, \ldots y_n) = \phi]$$

using '=' rather than '≡'.

[12]This is discussed more thoroughly in Jung [1994] and the issues are presented in Hatcher ([1968], 126).

the inadequacy of the notation as it stands, and since they didn't make use of circumflex abstracts in their actual derivations, therefore they tried to avoid its use in the body of PM.

The system of r-types alone provides the resources to resolve some of the paradoxes, even without consideration of comprehension axioms. There is no problem with the property "does not apply to itself", as any predicate F that represented it would have to be assigned an r-type, say $(\beta)/n$, and since that r-type can't be the same as, or directly lower than, the β of its arguments, neither $F(F)$ nor $\sim F(F)$ is well-formed. The paradoxical predicate can't be defined. Thus the classification of functions and arguments into different types is directly guaranteed by the formation rules of the language for the logic.

Other paradoxes are resolved in a less direct fashion. In each case producing a formal contradiction requires establishing the existence of a propositional function, or a proposition with certain properties that lead to contradiction. Above the problematic property is "does not apply to itself". The defining condition for this property is just not well-formed, according to the theory of types. In other cases some function or proposition seemingly can be defined, but careful attention to its type will show that the feared contradiction cannot be derived because the propositional function or proposition will not have the right type.

We will see below that the solution the theory of types offers for some paradoxes is just like that of axiomatic set theory. Axiomatic set theory postulates the existence of only certain sets by means of a restricted comprehension principle. Paradoxes such as the Russell Paradox of the set of all sets which are not members of themselves simply turn into proofs that no such set exists, that certain predicates do not correspond with sets. In a similar way, the system of types is supplemented with principles that assert the existence of propositional functions and propositions satisfying certain conditions. In this formulation some paradoxes turn out to be proofs that no function or proposition has certain purported properties. We will see in §5.5 below the example of how the theory of types turns Grelling's paradox into a proof that there is no "designation" relation of a certain purported kind. In such cases the offending or "paradoxical" notion is not in itself a violation of the theory of types, but, since it is not a theorem of the system that it does exist, the contradiction can be seen as a proof by *reductio ad absurdum* that there is no such thing. The theory of types does not solve all the paradoxes simply by ruling them ungrammatical, or violations of type restrictions.

The remainder of this chapter will be devoted to formalizing three more of Russell's examples, one symbolization and two paradoxes, which will help to illustrate both how the type system works and how, according to it, paradox is avoided. Consider first Russell's example of a higher order propositional function, "$\hat{x}$ has all the qualities that make for a great general" ([PM], 56). His formalization of this function might proceed by first introducing the predicate constant '$Q^{((\iota)/1)/1}$', which says of a first level (predicative) function that it is a quality which is part of the makings of a great general. To say then that x has all the qualities that make for a great general will require saying that x has all the properties of type $(\iota)/1$ that satisfy Q:[13]

$$(\forall f^{(\iota)/1})[Q^{((\iota)/1)/1}f \supset fx]$$

The relevant instance of the comprehension principle asserting the existence of a higher order (level 2) propositional function coextensive with '$\hat{x}$ has all the qualities that make for a great general' will then be:

$$(\exists h^{(\iota)/2})(\forall x^{\iota})\{hx \equiv (\forall f^{(\iota)/1})[Q^{((\iota)/1)/1}f \supset fx]\}$$

A second illustration of the effect of levels of r-types is Russell's account of the Paradox of the Liar:

> The oldest contradiction of this kind is the *Epimenides*. Epimenides the Cretan said that all Cretans were liars, and all other statements made by Cretans were certainly lies. Was this a lie? The simplest form of this contradiction is afforded by the man who says "I am lying"; if he is lying, he is speaking the truth, and vice versa. ([PM], 60)

In his analysis of the paradox Russell says that "I am lying" should be analyzed as "There is a proposition which I am affirming and which is false" ([PM], 62).

Symbolize that last assertion with constants 'A' for the relation of affirming and 'α' for the indexical 'I' as:

$$(\exists p^{(\ )/1})[A^{(\iota,(\ )/1)/1}(\alpha^{\iota},p) \wedge \sim p]$$

The theory of types requires that "There is a proposition . . ." must be restricted to "There is a proposition of type β . . .". A formal derivation of the paradox will require a premise that the only proposition affirmed is that very one, call it q. But q must be of a higher order than the one said to be false. The relevant instance of the comprehension principle will be:

$$(\exists q^{(\ )/2})\{q = (\exists p^{(\ )/1})[A^{(\iota,(\ )/1)/1}(\alpha^{\iota},p) \wedge \sim p]\}$$

---

[13]In symbolizations that follow the type of a variable or constant will be indicated only at its first occurrence, and occasionally type symbols ι for individuals will be omitted.

But now no contradiction results from premises asserting that q is the one and only false first order proposition affirmed, and so on, however the derivation of a contradiction is supposed then to proceed.

The resolution of the Epimenides paradox relies on the ramification of the theory of types, the division of functions of a given type of argument into different levels, and thus different orders. It also seems to require the use of variables ranging over propositions, something many have considered incompatible with the multiple relation theory. As noted before, however, Russell suggests that avoiding propositional variables is a matter of economy rather than an assertion of ontological commitment. The place of the Epimenides paradox in PM supports the contention of this work that propositions, even though denoted by "incomplete symbols", are envisaged as part of PM's ontology.

4.2   THE PARADOX OF PROPOSITIONS

As a final example illustrating the system of r-types, consider the paradox that Russell presents in Appendix B to *Principles of Mathematics* (§500, 527):

> Let us state the new contradiction more fully. If m be a class of propositions, the proposition "every m is true" may or may not be itself an m. But there is a one–one relation of this proposition to m: if n be different from m , "every n is true" is not the same proposition as "every m is true". Consider now the whole class of propositions of the form "every m is true", and having the property of not being members of their respective m's. Let this class be w, and let p be the proposition "every w is true". If p is a w, it must possess the defining property of w; but this property demands that p should not be a w. On the other hand, if p be not a w, then p does possess the defining property of w, and therefore is a w. Thus the contradiction appears unavoidable.

This paradox, which is less familiar than the paradox of the class of all classes that are not members of themselves, and the "semantic" paradoxes of Richard and Berry, is of crucial importance for understanding the development of the theory of types. It does use the notion of "truth" and classes of propositions, but is neither a set theoretic paradox nor a "semantic" paradox, and thus provides a counterexample to Ramsey's prominent account of the paradoxes. In his 1925 essay "The Foundations of Mathematics", Ramsey ([1965], 1–61) proposed that the paradoxes come in two kinds, those strictly "logical", which are to be resolved by the simple theory of types for classes, and "epistemological"

or "semantical" paradoxes that are due to additional nonlogical premises
from contentious domains, such as semantics. The solution of these latter paradoxes, he said, is not the job of logic alone, but will rely on a
satisfactory account of the semantic properties of sentences and of belief and knowledge. The notion of truth used in this paradox, however,
applies to propositions and not sentences that need semantic interpretation. Indeed this paradox is less plausibly seen as metalinguistic than
even a formulation of the Epimenides paradox in terms of asserting a
false proposition. The paradox in Appendix B, however, is about propositions and propositional functions and classes of them, not sentences or
predicates, and it has nothing to do with the relations between sentences
or predicates and those propositions and classes. Russell interpreted this
paradox as requiring the ramification of the simple theory of types that
he had just proposed in the preceding Appendix B to PoM as a first try
at a solution to the paradoxes. Russell describes this paradox in a letter
to Frege in 1902 and then says that it requires "... that not only functions but also ranges of values belong to different types", so requiring
that entities of the same simple type will have to be distinguished by
further types.[14] Contrary to Ramsey, then, one paradox, at least, was
neither to be resolved in the simple theory of types nor in the special
subject of semantics, but directly in a ramified theory of logical types.

The paradox presents a construction like that used in Cantor's proof
or the Russell paradox to show that there is no legitimate totality of
propositions. The argument is that if such a totality existed there would
be as many propositions as classes of propositions, yet a simple construction produces a proposition or class which is missed by any given
correlation. The proof uses the assumption that for every class of propositions m there will be another proposition "every m is true" thus making
possible a one–one correspondence between propositions and classes of
propositions. Russell only briefly notes the assumption that if classes
m and m' are different, then so are the propositions "every m is true"
and "every m' is true". He suggests, however, a view of propositions
as composed of constituents and very finely individuated by intensional
criteria. It is the simple non-identity of the classes involved that distinguishes the propositions, and so the classes themselves seem to enter
into the propositions as constituents. As well, this is an intensional view
of propositions, distinguishing some propositions that might well be materially equivalent. Both features remain in the later logic of PM.

---

[14]Letter from Russell to Frege of 29 September, 1902, in Frege ([1980], 147–148).
This paradox is discussed by L. Linsky [1983] and Goldfarb [1989] as providing reasons
for the ramification, and proof that Russell intended to construct an intensional logic.

It is necessary to formulate the paradox by treating m as a propositional function true of propositions, rather than as its extension, which is a class of propositions.[15] (In PoM the notions of function and class are not as clearly distinguished as they are later, after the "no-class" theory). Thus 'p is an m' could be formalized as '$p \in m$' rather than '$m(p)$' and the argument would be similarly analyzed. Then we are asked to consider the propositional function $w(\hat{q})$ such that:

$$(\forall q)\{w(q) \equiv (\exists m)(q = [(\forall s)(m(s) \supset s)]\wedge \sim m(q))\}$$

Now let:

$$p = (\forall s)(w(s) \supset s)$$

Then consider whether or not $w(p)$. If $w(p)$ then

$$(\exists m)\{p = [(\forall s)(m(s) \supset s)]\wedge \sim m(p)\}$$

each such predicate m yielding a different proposition. Hence if

$$p = [(\forall s)(m(s) \supset s)]$$

and

$$p = [(\forall s)(w(s) \supset s)]$$

then

$$m = w$$

(Note that an extensional notion of propositional identity might not guarantee this.) We can thus deduce that:

$$p = [(\forall s)(w(s) \supset s)]\wedge \sim w(p)$$

But then $\sim w(p)$. On the other hand, it follows that if $\sim w(p)$ then:

$$(\exists m)\{p = [(\forall s)(m(s) \supset s)]\wedge \sim m(p)\}$$

and so by the definition of w we derive $w(p)$, a contradiction.

The solution to this paradox comes with the introduction of orders (or levels) into the theory of types, its "ramification". The formula $w(p)$ which leads to paradox will then not be well-formed because of the rules on r-types. Consider first the r-type of w, which is guaranteed to exist subject to the restrictions on the comprehension principle:

$$(\forall q^{(\ )/1})\{w^{((\ )/1)/2}(q) \equiv$$
$$(\exists m^{((\ )/1)/1})(q = [(\forall s^{(\ )/1})(m(s) \supset s)] \wedge \sim m(q))\}$$

This w is defined in terms of the bound variable $m^{((\ )/1)/1}$ and so must be of type $((\ )/1)/2$ at least. Then consider the result of using a comprehension principle to define p:

$$p^{(\ )/3} = (\forall s^{(\ )/1})(w^{((\ )/1)/2}(s) \supset s)$$

---

[15] This formulation follows Church [1984], which provides axioms for propositional identity that may be added to PM to formulate the paradox.

p can only be a proposition of at least level 3 because it is defined in terms of w which is a propositional function of order 3. But then w is only defined for arguments which are propositions of level 1. If w were to be defined over propositions of level 3, ie. of type ( )/3, then it would have to be a function of type (( )/3)/2, thus order 5, and so p would have to be of even higher level, and so on. w simply cannot apply to p because of type restrictions and so the contradiction is avoided.

4.3   OTHER FORMULATIONS

In PM, Whitehead and Russell do not have a notation for types attached to their theorems. Rather, they treat the formulas as "typically ambiguous", containing free variables ranging over propositional functions which are to be interpreted so as to be well-formed according to the theory of types. Each theorem encapsulates an infinite class of theorems, repeated for each type.[16] This lack of explicit type symbols, and the vacillation that Russell experienced over what functions to treat as predicative (discussed below), has led some to the view that there is an unclarity about details of the the theory of types and that there might in fact be many different ways to make it precise. In this section I briefly describe some of the formulations of the theory of types that have been proposed to indicate what is in fact the very slight extent of the variations among them. The differences are generally due to the collapse of some type distinctions that can be made, such as making the types cumulative, or even obliterating some distinctions altogether. The full ramified theory of types is very finely divided. The purposes of foundations of mathematics, served by the axiom of reducibility and axioms of extensionality about sets, undo many of the distinctions in the full theory. Thus the variants of the theory of types range along a scale (though perhaps not a linear ordering). They can be ordered according to how many distinctions they observe. Church's system is maximal in that regard, and will be used as a schema for representing the other formulations that follow.

Irving Copi ([1971], chapter 3) presents the ramified theory of types as simply adding a second dimension to the hierarchy of the simple theory of types:

> One dimension of the Ramified Theory is the Simple Theory of Types, which suffices to avoid the logical paradoxes as explained in Chapter 2.

---

[16]These variables have been interpreted as both schematic letters and as genuine variables, with appropriate adjustments elsewhere in the system, for example in Church [1976] and Jung [1994].

The other dimension of the Ramified Theory of Types cuts right across the Simple Type Theory. For each type, the functions of that type are divided further into infinitely many *orders*. ([1971], 82–83)

He considers the functions of a single argument and then lays out a grid, with rows representing types and columns the different orders. Thus one row consists of functions of an argument of a given type divided by columns into orders:

$$\text{Order 1} \qquad\qquad \text{Order 2} \qquad\qquad \text{Order 3} \qquad \ldots$$

$$\vdots \qquad\qquad\qquad \vdots \qquad\qquad\qquad \vdots \qquad\qquad \vdots$$

type 3: $^1F^3, ^1G^3, ^1H^3 \ldots; \ ^2F^3, ^2G^3, ^2H^3, \ldots; \ ^3F^3, ^3G^3, ^3H^3, \ldots; \ldots$

type 2: $^1F^2, ^1G^2, ^1H^2 \ldots; \ ^2F^2, ^2G^2, ^2H^2, \ldots; \ ^3F^2, ^3G^2, ^3H^2, \ldots; \ldots$

type 1: $^1F^1, ^1G^1, ^1H^1 \ldots; \ ^2F^1, ^2G^1, ^2H^1, \ldots; \ ^3F^1, ^3G^1, ^3H^1, \ldots; \ldots$

The right superscript indicates what Copi calls the "type" (hereafter "c-type") of the argument, the left the "order" ("c-order") of the function. Different functions with arguments of a given c-type, say 2, will have differing r-types as arguments, thus functions with arguments of the differing r-types $((\iota)/1)$, $((\iota)/2)$, etc. will all be of c-type 2. This follows Copi's idea that the simple type theory is merely ramified in a second dimension. The c-type of a function is just the *simple type* of its arguments plus one. (The "simple type" can be determined from r-types by erasing all the level indications ' $/n$', then counting ι as of simple-type 0, (ι) of simple type 1, $((\iota))$ of simple type 2, etc.)

The relation of Copi's c-order to r-types is not so directly obvious. It might even seem that Copi's classification is simply incorrect, since he allows that the c-order of a function can be lower than its c-type. (This is claimed by Landini [1996] to be a failing of Copi's account.) Clearly, however, since c-orders begin at 1 again in each c-type, they are closer to Church's notion of level than order. Suppose, then, that in the conversion from r-types to Copi's "types", we let the level of the r-type be the c-order. Some examples comparing r-types and Copi types will make this clear: $((\iota)/1)/1$ belongs to $^1F^2$, $((\iota)/2)/1$ to $^1F^2$ as well, and $((\iota)/1)/2$ to $^2F^2$. Thus Copi seems simply to identify what would be distinct r-types for Church. Does this identification ever violate the vicious circle principle? Clearly a function will always be of a different "type" from its arguments; indeed it will always be of the next highest c-type. The second order property of having all the qualities of a great general, discussed above, which is of r-type $(\iota)/2$, will be of the type of Copi's $^2F^1$, and so on, for all such impredicative definitions. Adopting instead Church's r-types as an account of types spoils the nice imagery of orders and types as orthogonal dimensions in the hierarchy of types. An attempt to characterize disagreements about the theory as simply a matter of whether types are divided into orders, or orders into types, will not be to the point. But that does not mean that oversimplified classifications, such as Copi's, necessarily reintroduce paradoxes. Rather they may be seen as overly coarse approximations which none the less enforce the restrictions of the vicious circle principle.

Looking ahead to interpretive problems with PM to be discussed in the next chapter, Copi seems to follow Russell's remarks in the introduction that all functions can be derived by generalization over predicative functions in a matrix. The relevant features of the type of a predicative function on that version are just the simple type of its arguments and its level. There couldn't be two predicative types of different levels. Pelham ([1993], chapter 4) also finds Copi's account congenial since it fits with her view that, carrying over from the earlier substitutional view that propositional functions are really nothing, the real objects of PM are individuals and perhaps propositions. Thus the types of functions as arguments aren't relevant to functions since they don't really appear as arguments.

William Hatcher ([1968], chapter 4) develops a system, **RT**, of ramified type theory that is intended to serve as a foundation of mathematics. It therefore includes an axiom of extensionality which is out of keeping with the system of PM as logic, as well as some other features that differ from Church's. Hatcher uses a formulation of comprehension principles solely in terms of abstracts, terms for propositional functions using the circumflex '$\hat{x}$' as a term forming operator, and a variant of lambda conversion: $(\forall y)(\phi\hat{x}(y) \equiv \phi y)$, instead of a comprehension axiom and a few similar differences. The type notation, however, makes the same distinctions of types as Church's formulation. He formally defines "*order-type*" symbols ([1968], 143) of the form '$(t_1, \ldots, t_n)/k/(y_1, \ldots, y_n)$'. The symbols '$(t_1, \ldots, t_n)$' are the types symbols for the arguments of the function symbolized: the 'k' represents the *order* of the function symbol and '$(y_1, \ldots, y_n)$' the respective orders of its arguments. The type symbols are defined inductively as follows: ... " 'o' is a type symbol (for individuals) and if $t_1, \ldots, t_n$ are all type symbols, then the expression $(t_1, \ldots, t_n)$ is also a type symbol (for the functions with $t_1, \ldots, t_n$ as arguments)" ([1968], 123). The *orders* are defined this way: " The type symbol 'o' is of order zero. A type symbol of the form $(o, \ldots, o)$ (all o's) is of order one. Inductively, a type symbol $(t_1, \ldots, t_k)$ is of order $n+1$ if the highest order of the type symbols t_i is n." ([1968], 127) The rest of the definition proceeds: "Finally, if a term A is an abstract, then let n be the highest order of all of its variables (bound or free) and constants. If there is a bound variable y of order n in A, then A is of order $n+1$. If not, then A is of order n (in this case A must have some free variable or a constant of order n). Let us recall that circumflexed variables are bound." (This is the manifestation of the requirement that a propositional function defined in terms of certain objects be of a higher order-type than those objects.)

Hatcher would represent the above sample r-type type symbol '$((\iota)/2, (\ )/2)/1$' in his notation as '$((o)(\ ))/3/(2,2)$'. The middle term in Hatcher's notation, then, is what Church calls the *order* of the symbol. What Church represents as the *level* (1 in this case) can be easily recovered from Hatcher's notation. Hatcher, however, only records the order of the arguments and not their full r-type. Thus consider functions of the following distinct r-types: $(((\iota)/1)/2)/1$ and $(((\iota)/2)/1)/1$. Hatcher would represent them with the same "order-type" symbol: '$(((o)))/1/3$'. That is because he only records the order of the argument of a function, not its r-type, which indicates the way in which that order was attained. We can thus have a predicative function of second level functions of predicative functions of individuals, or a predicative function of predicative functions of second level functions of individuals. Both will be predicative, of order 4, and have as arguments functions of functions of functions of individuals, but will differ as to r-type. Hatcher's symbol only tells us that we have a function of functions of functions of individuals, that it is predicative, and that its argument is of order 3.

Copi's system specifies the type of a function in terms of the simple type of its arguments and the number of levels higher that are quantified over in the definition of the function. Hatcher uses Copi-types (c-types and c-orders) to describe the arguments of the function and adds another index for the level of the quantifiers used in the specification of the function, the c-order of the function. Church's system goes all the way, specifying those features of the arguments of the functions, the arguments of those arguments, etc, all the way down. If one is interested solely in blocking the paradoxes, then a system like Copi's is fine grained enough. Hatcher is interested in developing predicative set theory and so is concerned with distinguishing the arguments of functions in terms of the quantifiers used to define them. The arguments of a function become the members of a predicative set in a logicist reconstruction of set theory. It is Church's approach, which is fully intensional, and sees propositional functions as individuated very finely by all of their constituents, which satisfies the desire to trace all of the dependencies of functions back to the totalities from which they are "constructed". As we shall see below, even Church's types do not record all of the elements in the structure of a propositional function, just the pattern of dependencies on entities, totalities of entities, totalities of totalities of entities, etc.

Finally, the systems of Chihara and Myhill, which, though superficially different, turn out to be equivalent to Church's. Their notations for types amounts to the same classification. There has simply not been the variation in interpretations of ramified types that one would have expected if the account in PM were vague or incomplete in some serious fashion.

Chihara ([1973], §1.5) repeats the charge that there are different versions of the theory of types even in PM and presents his own formulation of the structure of types, using functions of a single argument as an example. (As with Hatcher, Chihara's interest is in developing a predicative theory of classes, so he thinks that only monadic functions will be necessary, but the extension to functions of arbitrary numbers of arguments would not be incompatible with the system).

> Individuals will be of type T_0. Propositional functions of order 1 will be of type T_1. Propositional functions of order 2 taking individuals as arguments will be of type $T_{2.0}$. Propositional functions of order 2 taking propositional functions of type T_1 as arguments will be of type $T_{2.1}$. In this way we can build up the hierarchy of types as follows:

$$\vdots$$

$$T_{4.0} \quad T_{4.1} \quad T_{4.2.0} \quad T_{4.2.1} \quad T_{4.3.0} \quad T_{4.3.1} \quad T_{4.3.2.0} \quad T_{4.3.2.1}$$

$$T_{3.0} \quad T_{3.1} \quad T_{3.2.0} \quad T_{3.2.1}$$

$$T_{2.0} \quad T_{2.1}$$

$$T_1$$

$$T_0$$

All the same types are distinguished as in Church's system of r-types. Consider Chihara's third order functions, for example:

$$T_{3.0}, \quad T_{3.1}, \quad T_{3.2.0}, \quad T_{3.2.1}$$

These are just Church's r-types:

$$(\iota)/3, \quad ((\iota)/1)/2, \quad ((\iota)/2)/1, \quad (((\iota)/1)/1)/1$$

Chihara's account of predicative functions seems to follow Church as well.[17] For Church a predicative function is one which has the lowest

---

[17]That of the introduction version rather than that of *12. See the discussion in

possible order compatible with the r-type of its arguments, i.e., it has level 1, and so has an order just one more than that of the arguments. Chihara says that predicative functions are of the sort T_1 or $T_{k,k-1,\sigma}$, where σ is a sequence "of the required sort" ([1973], 22) (i.e. a series of types beginning with something less than $k-1$). The step from $k-1$ to k is the same increment of 1.[18]

John Myhill [1979] gives another notational variant. He presents a system "Ramified Principia" (RP), which with an axiom of reducibility becomes the system "PM". Myhill uses the system of types in Schütte ([1960], 245–247) and adds his own formulation of the axioms. I will call these "Myhill-Schütte types" or "ms-types". The system also includes levels, "ms-levels". Types can be defined as follows: 0, the type of individuals, is an ms-type of *level* 0. $m(\ )$ is the ms-type of propositions of ms-level m. If $\sigma_1,\ldots,\sigma_n$ are ms-types then $m(\sigma_1,\ldots,\sigma_n)$ is an ms-type of ms-level m, provided that m is greater than the maximum of the ms-levels of $\sigma_1,\ldots,\sigma_n$. $m(\sigma_1,\ldots,\sigma_n)$ is intended to be the ms-type of functions with n arguments of ms-types $\sigma_1,\ldots,\sigma_n$ whose arguments do not "involve" quantification over any ms-types of ms-level greater than or equal to m.

The terms are (i) the variables, (ii) atomic formulas $f(t_1,\ldots,t_n)$ (of ms-level m) when f is a term of ms-type $m(\sigma_1,\ldots,\sigma_n)$ and $t_1,\ldots,t_n$ are terms of the appropriate ms-types $\sigma_1,\ldots,\sigma_n$, and (iii) abstracts $\phi\hat{x}_1\ldots\hat{x}_n$ (also of ms-level m) where ϕ is a formula of ms-level m, and $\hat{x}_1\ldots\hat{x}_n$ are of ms-types $\sigma_1,\ldots,\sigma_n$.

Atomic Formulas are the variables, terms $f(t_1,\ldots t_n)$, and $t_1 = t_2$ (of the ms-level of t_1 and t_2) where t_1 and t_2 are of the same ms-type.

Other formulas are built up with connectives in the usual way, having ms-levels of the maximum of the ms-levels of their subformulas and quantified formulas $(\forall x)\phi$ having the least ms-level which is greater than the ms-level of x and no less than the ms-level of ϕ.

This system, RP, is axiomatized with many-sorted predicate calculus,

---

the next chapter.

[18]Chihara goes on to say ([1973], 45), however, that most of these predicative types do not make a difference with respect to set theory; indeed, only the types T_0, T_1, $T_{2.1}$, $T_{3.2.1}$, $T_{4.3.2.1}$, etc, are "crucial", which leads to the conclusion that in so far as it proves the existence of sets, the ramified theory of types is no proper extension of the simple theory of types. A type such as $T_{2.0}$ will not guarantee the existence of any new sets beyond those of T_1. The sets of individuals defined with propositional functions of order 2 are just the same as the sets defined with functions of order 1, and so sets of, say, type $T_{3.2.0}$ will be the same as those at type $T_{3.0}$, the same as those of type T_1, etc. If we deny the existence of intensional propositional functions, then the axiom of reducibility does seem to amount to a claim that only simple types are predicative, but, as Chihara sees, that is not what the axiom says.

with identity, together with the (conversion) schema:[19]

$$\phi \hat{x}_1 \ldots \hat{x}_n(x_1, \ldots, x_n) \equiv \phi$$

This system of type indicators is also a notational variant of Church's. Myhill uses ms-levels to record what is for Church the "order" of a function. Church's levels can be recovered as the increments in ms-levels. Consider two of the sample r-types I have been discussing and their equivalents in ms-types. $(((\iota)/1)/2)/1$ becomes $4(3(1(0)))$ and $(((\iota)/2)/1)/1$ becomes $4(3(2(0)))$. The difference between successive ms-levels is precisely the "level" in the corresponding r-type. ms-levels are simply a running count of the calculation of the order of a function. The rest of the system PM is effectively equivalent to Church's formulation as well. Where Church requires an increase in level in functions defined by quantifiers in the comprehension schema, Myhill builds that requirement into the requirement of ms-level on abstracts. This is what prevents the vicious circle paradoxes. Clearly a function will be of a higher ms-level than its arguments, the other requirement of a type system.

---

[19]To get the full system of *Principia*, called PM, add the axiom of reducibility presented this way:

$$(\exists f_{m(\sigma_1, \ldots, \sigma_n)})(\forall x_1) \ldots (\forall x_n) f(x_1, \ldots, x_n) \equiv \phi$$

where $x_1, \ldots, x_n$ are of ms-types $\sigma_1, \ldots, \sigma_n$ respectively, ϕ is of arbitrary ms-level and m exceeds by 1 the maximum of the ms-levels of $\sigma_1, \ldots, \sigma_n$.

5

TYPES IN *Principia Mathematica*

The theory of types in *Principia Mathematica* is defended in the introduction, written principally by Russell, and in the introductory sections to each number. These contain both Russell's justification for the restrictions imposed by the "vicious circle principle" and his account of the ensuing classification of functions into logical types. These discussions have led to several problems for interpreting PM, both challenges to the justifications that Russell provides, and apparently different details of the structure of the theory of types in different passages. In what follows I will try to provide an account of the metaphysical insight behind the vicious circle principle and use that account to resolve the interpretive problems.

5.1   THE VICIOUS CIRCLE PRINCIPLE

The basis of the justification for the theory of types is the "vicious circle principle". Russell provides three versions of the principle in the introduction to PM:

> More generally, given any set of objects such that, if we suppose the set to have a total, it will contain members which presuppose this total, then such a set cannot have at total. By saying that a set has "no total", we mean, primarily, that no significant statement can be made about "all its members". ([PM], 37)

Later, on that same page, we find two more versions in one sentence:

> The principle which enables us to avoid illegitimate totalities may be stated as follows: "Whatever involves *all* of a collection must not be one of the collection"; or conversely: "If, provided a certain collection had a total, it would have members only definable in terms of that total, then the said collection has no total." ([PM], 37)

The expressions "presupposing", "involving", and being "only definable in terms of" are not synonymous. Gödel [1944] and Quine [1963] charge that if one is a realist the vicious circle principle should be denied in the version using "involving", and that the principle should only be held true if one is a constructivist and the principle is stated using "definable only in terms of". Quine ([1963], 243) uses the example of "the most typical Yale man" (echoing Ramsey's original example "the tallest man in the group").[1] Here we legitimately pick out an individual in terms of a group to which he belongs. There is no vicious circle because the men all exist prior to any "definition" or "identification" by a description. Thus, say Quine and Gödel, if we are realists about entities there is no legitimate reason to ban impredicative specification of them.[2] On the other hand, if we think that the objects are constructed in the very act of identification or definition, then it would be legitimate to ban impredicative definitions. They conclude that one cannot both be a realist about entities and ban impredicative specification of those entities.

The notions of presupposing, depending on, etc., that are used to explain vicious circularity are really metaphysical notions of dependence. The vicious circle principle expresses the metaphysical intuition behind the notion of well-foundedness, as expressed in set theory by the axiom of foundation. Chains of dependence must come to an end. a cannot depend on b, b on c, c on d, and so on, without end. The supposedly "constructivist" tinge in the vicious-circle principle also has a parallel in set theory. The "iterative conception" of sets describes the platonistic universe of sets with non-sets or *ur-elements* as members as though it were constructed in stages. V_0, the first stage, is just the set A of ur-elements. V_1 is the set of V_0's subsets, i.e., just $\wp A$; V_2, is its power set, $\wp(\wp A)$; etc. In general, $V_{\alpha+1}$ is "constructed" from V_α by the "operation" of taking the power set, taking the union of the previous V_n at limit ordinals ω and beyond. The whole universe of sets is built by iterating

---

[1] The example is in Ramsey's *The Foundations of Mathematics* [1965]. Gödel [1944] refers to it in his discussion of "Russell's Mathematical Logic". I will refer to the tallest man in *the room*.

[2] The term 'impredicative' has three related uses. It was originally used by Russell to identify those functions that do not pick out classes. Following Poincaré's criticism of vicious circles, it has come to identify the use of quantifiers defining an object which range over that object itself. This common use is to be distinguished from Russell's own use of the term for a a function of lowest possible order compatible with its arguments. The theory of types bans "impredicative" definitions in the second sense, while allowing functions that aren't predicative in the third. The first use is preserved in the "no-class" theory, in that the only functions that replace classes are predicative in the third sense.

this operation through all the ordinals. Yet we need not see the sets as constructed by the act of definition in any way; the hierarchy of sets merely captures the structure of the universe of sets and the structure of each set in it. It is sometimes quite natural to express metaphysical notions of ontological dependency and of rank in this way, as though they were the results of a stage by stage construction. Constructivist talk by Russell should be taken in the same way as in the iterative conception. Indeed the structure of the iterative conception helps to make sense of some of the rival accounts of the theory of types to be discussed below. If we think of a predicative function of type $(\iota)/1$ as depending on its arguments, then the functions of that type presuppose V_0, the set of all individuals at the bottom of the hierarchy. A function defined in terms of quantifiers ranging over properties of type $(\iota)/1$ will presuppose their totality, and so will be of r-type $(\iota)/2$ and depend on V_1. As we shall see below, however, the theory of types is not a theory of sets and other extensional entities; it includes intensional propositional functions, so the simple hierarchy of the iterative conception does not represent all of its structure.

The different expressions of the vicious circle principle suggest different aspects of the theory of types, even though they come from a common idea.[3] Type restrictions show up twice in formulations of the theory of types. One place is in the conditions on well-formed formulas. The order of a function f which applies to terms $t_1, t_2, \ldots, t_n$ must be at least one more than the largest order of $t_1, t_2, \ldots, t_n$. This is the feature that rules out talk of a property applying (or not applying) to itself. Type restrictions also show up in the comprehension principle, which holds only if the order of the function f, which the principle guarantees to exist, is higher than the order of any of the bound variables in the specifying ϕ. This restriction holds because whatever is presupposed by the variables in ϕ is also presupposed by f. Darryl Jung [1994] has suggested that these two restrictions arise from two different formulations of the vicious circle principle, the first from the formulation in terms of "presupposing" and the second from that using "definable in terms of". A function presupposes its arguments for Russell and so must be of a different type from its arguments. Russell puts the sort of dependence expressed in comprehension principles in terms of what is "definable" in certain ways.[4]

---

[3]Pointed out by Jung [1994].

[4]This version of the vicious circle principle is most explicit in the formulation in OI (198): "Whatever involves an apparent variable must not be among the values of that variable".

Quine may have intended some irony with his use of the definite description "the most typical Yale man" to raise a difficulty for Russell. Quine was clearly alluding to Russell's own account of definite descriptions, such as the use of a proper description in "The present Queen of England is bald". That description will be analyzed away as "There is a person who is a queen of England and is such that *any person* who is a present queen of England is identical with her and she is bald." Thus the description denotes Elizabeth in terms of a quantifier ranging over all persons. Clearly *all* proper definite descriptions "denote" an individual in terms of a totality of which that individual is a member. Why is there no violation of the vicious circle principle in such cases? Is it simply because we are realists about people, so that the only way one would sense a violation of the principle is if one is dealing with constructions? That is not the only possible account.

We should distinguish between factual sentences expressing identities and instances of comprehension principles.

(1) $(\imath y^{\iota})[InRoom(y) \wedge (\forall z^{\iota})(InRoom(z) \supset Tallas(y, z))]$

expresses 'the tallest (person) in the room'.[5] When we say that someone exists who is the tallest in the room we get:

(2) $(\exists x^{\iota})\{x = (\imath y^{\iota})[InRoom(y) \wedge (\forall z^{\iota})(InRoom(z) \supset Tallas(y, z))]\}$

The question that Quine and Ramsey raise amounts to asking why the order of x should be that of individuals in (2), while in the comprehension principle for propositional functions there is an increase in order. It would seem that if the variables on the right hand side of (2) presuppose the totality of individuals, then so does that on the left. The difference is that (2) is not an instance of a comprehension principle. Comprehension principles are special, but not because they show how an entity is constructed, as Quine and Gödel think. Rather it is that comprehension principles reveal the metaphysical structure of propositional functions in a way that other ways of describing entities do not.

The example of a definite description above might seem irrelevant, for it concerns individuals, which do not divide into orders, rather than comprehension principles for propositional functions, which do. But of course there can be higher order descriptions as well. Consider the instance of the comprehension principle guaranteeing the existence of the propositional function '($\hat{x}$ has the brightest color in the room)', where that is analyzed as saying that x has a color which is as bright as any color in the room. Using symbols '$C^{((\iota)/1)/1}$' for 'is a color in the room', a property of first order properties, and '$B^{((\iota)/1,(\iota)/1)/1}$' for the relation

---

[5] Where that means a person "as tall as" any in the room.

of first order properties 'is as bright as' and with superscripts added to indicate types we get:

(3) $(\exists f^{(\iota)/2})(\forall x^{\iota})\{f(x) \equiv$
$$(\forall h^{(\iota)/1})(\forall g^{(\iota)/1})[g(x) \wedge C(g) \wedge C(h) \supset B(h, g)]\}$$

Compare this with the assertion that there is some brightest color in the room:

(4) $(\exists f^{(\iota)/1})\{f = (\imath g^{(\iota)/1})[C(g) \wedge \forall h^{(\iota)/1}(C(h) \supset B(h, g)]\}$

The Quine/Gödel/Ramsey problem becomes this: given that the variables g and h on the righthand side of (4) range over all predicative first order propositional functions, those of type $(\iota)/1$, why doesn't the function on the left then depend on them all and hence become of type $(\iota)/2$? The answer is that (3) is an instance of a comprehension principle, the propositional function is "only definable in terms of" the expression on the right, which presents its analysis. Sentence (4) merely picks out a preexisting propositional function and identifies it in terms of its features.

Propositional functions are functions, but they are also structured entities. With some conceptions of functions, such as Frege's view of those he called "concepts", which are functions from objects to truth values, one cannot recover the argument of a function from its value. Propositional functions are different, however. A function $\hat{x}Rb$ will have the value aRb for argument a. The structure of the function, including its constituents R and b, is carried along into the proposition which is its value.[6] Unlike a definite description, a comprehension principle will show the structure of the function being defined, and so shows what that function presupposes. Its type must be as high as any of its constituents.

5.2 PREDICATIVE FUNCTIONS AND MATRICES

What system of types should we attribute to PM? That work relies on the device of "typical ambiguity" to avoid introducing explicit symbols for types. Types are to be thought of as added in a way compatible with the theory as needed to produce instances of each axiom. What if we wish to make these type indicators explicit? What is the structure of the theory of types that should be represented in the indicators?

As Church ([1976], 747) points out, the paradoxes are avoided if quantification over a domain does not add new members to the domain. All of the systems discussed in the last chapter guarantee that the comprehension principle will assign different types to a function and its arguments,

---

[6]See Hylton [1993] for the differences between this notion of a propositional function and Frege's notion of a concept as a function.

and to a propositional function and another introduced by means of a quantifier that ranges over the first. In the preface ([PM], vii) Russell says that other systems of types can also ban the paradoxes, and that aside from explicit discussion of types, not much in the work depends on the particular theory of types that is adopted.

In contemporary logic, however, it would be unthinkable to propose a theory of types without making it completely specific. In part this is due to the syntactic approach to logic, by which a logic must be presented as a formal system, and type indicators of some sort would be essential to the formalism. The whole issue of what propositional functions there are and what types they fall into would be represented in the symbolism for functions and in explicitly stated comprehension principles. That Russell does not proceed in this fashion, and seems even to change his mind in various places, has given rise to several interpretive problems about identifying the "real" system of types in PM.

Below I will distinguish three issues about the system of types in PM, although they are interrelated and solutions have been proposed that are not independent of each other. To begin with, there does not even seem to be a unique system presented in the work. Church identifies two, one present in Russell [1908] and the "Introduction" to the first edition of PM, another in *12 and the "Introduction to the Second Edition".[7] As evidence for his claim Church cites Russell's statement in the *Preface* that:

> The explanation of the hierarchy of types in the introduction differs slightly from that given in *12 of the body of the work. The latter explanation is stricter and is that which is assumed throughout the rest of the book. ([PM], vii)

Russell does not say more about the differences between the systems, but discussion since has concentrated on the account of predicative functions and matrices as the most likely interpretation of his remark.

In the introduction ([PM], 50) Russell defines a *matrix* as a function that contains no "apparent" (bound) variables. He lists the examples of functions $\phi(x, y)$, $(y).\phi(x, y)$, $(x).\phi(x, y)$, and $(x, y).\phi(x, y)$, (all of which are *first order*), and identifies the first as a matrix. A matrix, then, is a function which does not contain quantifiers. (Russell also uses the notion of an *elementary* function, but does not explicitly distinguish elementary

---

[7] Church [1976] identifies his own system in as yet a third, but the differences are not in the individuation of type symbols. Church introduces orders and levels where Russell only uses "order" and in makes both orders and levels cumulative. As well there are the variations dealing with abstracts and comprehension principles noted above.

functions and matrices. From what he says it appears that an elementary function is an atomic matrix.)

Immediately we are told that:

> It is thus plain that all possible propositions and functions are obtainable from matrices by the process of turning the arguments to the matrices into apparent variables.

Functions, then, can be analyzed into the matrices from which they are derived by binding quantifiers.

At PM (51) we find *first-order* functions defined as those that involve "no variables except individuals", i.e., individual variables. He then introduces the notation $\phi!\hat{x}$ for these functions. (This is the notation he later uses for *predicative functions* in general and is thus a source of more confusion.)

Similarly a *second order* matrix is defined ([PM], 52) as one such as $F(\phi!\hat{z}, x)$ which contains individuals and first order functions as arguments, but contains no apparent variables.

A *second order* function is "such as contain variables that are first-order functions, but contain no other variables except (possibly) individuals". (To "contain a variable" presumably means to take the value of a *real* or free variable as an argument.) Predicative functions f of first-order functions having values for an argument ϕ such as $(\forall x).\phi!x$ and $(\exists x).\phi!x$ and ϕa (for a a constant) are "predicative functions of first order functions" and are written '$f!(\hat{\phi}!\hat{z})$'.

At PM (53) we find that a *predicative* function is "of the next order above that of its argument, *i.e.* of the lowest order compatible with its having that argument". By the above definition, then, every first order function will be a predicative function of individuals, since it is of the lowest order (first) compatible with its arguments, but only some second and higher order functions will be predicative.

So far we have an account that is compatible with Church's formulation (excepting the use of the notation $\phi!\hat{x}$ to mean "first order function" rather than "predicative", though for first order functions the two notions are coextensive).

Now for the first problem involving predicative functions and matrices. At PM (53–54) we find:

> And speaking generally, a non-predicative function of the nth order is obtained from a predicative function of the nth order by turning all the arguments of the $n-1$th order into apparent variables. (Other arguments also may be turned into apparent variables.)

This much is compatible with Church's account. Immediately, however, he says:

> Thus we need not introduce as variables any functions except predicative functions.

It seems that some non predicative functions are being ignored. Which non predicative functions can there be? This is the first of the issues concerning the system of PM which we will consider. This thesis about the form of all possible functions is explicitly repeated a few lines later at PM (54):

> Thus speaking generally, by a succession of steps we find that, if $\phi!\hat{u}$ is a predicative function of sufficiently high order, any assigned non-predicative function of x will be of one of the two forms:
>
> $$(\phi).F!(\phi!\hat{u}, x), (\exists\phi).F!(\phi!\hat{u}, x)$$
>
> where F is a predicative function of $\phi!\hat{u}$ and x.

This claim that all functions can be derived by quantifying over predicative functions runs contrary to Church's account. It would seem that ϕ, above, need not be predicative. We should be able to define some function only with an expression $(\forall\phi).F!(\phi\hat{u}, x)$ or $(\exists\phi).F!(\phi\hat{u}, x)$ where ϕ is not predicative.

Consider an example presented by Hylton ([1990], 309), for which he thanks Thomas G. Ricketts. Start with the following two (partially symbolized) sentences:

> $(\forall x)(x$ is a great general $\supset x$ is brave) $\wedge$ Smith is brave.

> $(\forall x)(x$ is a great general $\supset x$ is decisive) $\wedge$ Jones is decisive.

Generalizing each we get:

> $(\exists\phi)((\forall x)(x$ is a great general $\supset \phi x) \wedge \phi$ Smith)

> $(\exists\phi)((\forall x)(x$ is a great general $\supset \phi x) \wedge \phi$ Jones)

So far we proceed as Russell says, producing new functions by binding apparent variables for predicative functions. However, we can also derive the following:

> $(\exists\psi)(\psi$ Smith $\wedge\psi$ Jones)

where the ψ in question is not derived solely from predicative functions, nor does it seem derivable from some other predicative functions.

A symbolized version of these inferences will show how they proceed using the notation of Church's r-types. Use the symbols '$G^{(\iota)/1}x$', '$B^{(\iota)/1}x$' and '$D^{(\iota)/1}x$' for the predicative functions '$\hat{x}$ is a great general', '$\hat{x}$ is brave' and '$\hat{x}$ is decisive', respectively, and 's^ι' and 'j^ι' as the individual constants for 'Smith' and 'Jones'. The first two sentences become:

$$(\forall x^\iota)(G^{(\iota)/1}x \supset B^{(\iota)/1}x) \wedge Bs^\iota$$

and

$$(\forall x^\iota)(G^{(\iota)/1}x \supset D^{(\iota)/1}x) \wedge Dj^\iota$$

Generalizing we get:

$$(\exists \phi^{(\iota)/1})[(\forall x^\iota)(G^{(\iota)/1}x \supset \phi x) \wedge \phi s^\iota]$$

and

$$(\exists \phi^{(\iota)/1})[(\forall x^\iota)(G^{(\iota)/1}x \supset \phi x) \wedge \phi j^\iota]$$

Abstracting 'Smith' and 'Jones':

$$\{(\exists \phi^{(\iota)/1})[(\forall x^\iota)(G^{(\iota)/1}x \supset \phi x) \wedge \phi \hat{y}^\iota]\}(s^\iota)$$

and

$$\{(\exists \phi^{(\iota)/1})[(\forall x^\iota)(G^{(\iota)/1}x \supset \phi x) \wedge \phi \hat{y}^\iota]\}(j^\iota)$$

yields a non-predicative function of type $(\iota)/2$, applied to s and j. Conjoining the two and generalizing again we arrive at the higher order function in the conclusion:

$$(\exists \psi^{(\iota)/2})(\psi s^\iota \wedge \psi j^\iota)$$

This ψ is a function which is not derived by quantifying over predicative functions. $(\exists \phi^{(\iota)/1})[(\forall x^\iota)(G^{(\iota)/1}x \supset \phi x) \wedge \phi \hat{y}^\iota]$ is of r-type $(\iota)/2$ and so is not of the lowest possible level compatible with its arguments, namely individuals. It appears that Russell has overlooked some ways of defining propositional functions.

Some treat Russell's claim about the form of all non predicative functions as more than an oversight. Hylton ([1990], 309) sees it as a view that is simply incompatible with what is said elsewhere in PM, one of several inconsistencies to bedevil the work. Landini [1996] uses this passage as evidence for his radical interpretation of "the real *Principia*", claiming that higher order bound variables range only over predicative functions, and that therefore Russell does not acknowledge anything in his ontology *but* predicative functions.[8]

---

[8]Landini [1996] and [1998] takes this as evidence that the bound variables of PM range *only* over predicative functions, that all talk of others should be taken as remarks about schematic formulas, in a metalinguistic way. The axiom of reducibility then is simply the only comprehension principle in PM. The three interpretive diffi-

While troubling, Russell's claim seems better interpreted as an oversight than as an expression of a startling logical doctrine. Russell clearly intends to show how the whole hierarchy of types is generated by an iterative process. For each type of argument, he thinks, we derive the ramification of the theory of types by quantifying over some variables. At each level a quantifier over all propositions or propositional functions raises the type of a proposition or function, even when its arguments are still of a lower type. Russell hypothesizes that this quantification, which requires a change in type to observe the vicious circle principle, is in fact minimal; it is the *only* way that higher order functions can be derived.

Russell sees higher types as obtained from just two sources: (i) matrices that have a lower type as argument, such as $F(\phi\hat{x}, y)$, which must be of a higher type than ϕ and (ii) by quantification; so, for example, $(\exists\phi)F(\phi\hat{x}, x)$ must be of a higher order than $F(\phi\hat{x}, y)$. What he overlooked is the role of abstraction in producing new functions. It is possible to abstract a function and then quantify over it. Thus in the above example what Smith and Jones share is a property that can only be derived by abstraction from a complex quantified formula. Abstracting from formulas built up by quantification over predicative functions and sentential connectives, and then quantifying, can produce functions which can't be derived by quantifying solely over predicative functions. In the above example, both being a great general and the two different instances of ϕ, being brave and being decisive, are predicative functions, but having some particular property possessed by all great generals is not predicative.[9]

This diagnosis of oversight is supported by the vacillation that seems to be involved with propositional connectives in quantified formulas, and results in the duplication of sections *9 and *10. In *9 Russell and Whitehead assume that connectives only apply to lowest order matrices, and then show how to find equivalents for any given formula which has all propositional connectives inside the scope of all the quantifiers, i.e., "prenex" form. Those equivalences show that axioms of propositional

---

culties in this section are in fact central to Landini's interpretation. In what follows I try to present them as minor anomalies rather than requiring the radical reinterpretation Landini provides.

[9] As Hatcher and Jung both point out, Russell makes a similiar error of forgetting some abstracted propositional functions in his account of the circumflex notation. To use Jung's example (where the superscripts indicate orders in an obvious fashion), $\lambda y^1(\pi^3 \lambda x^1(xL^2y))$ involves different functions from $\lambda x^1(\pi^3 \lambda y^1(x^1L^2y^1))$, yet both would seemingly be represented with the same formula $\hat{x}L\hat{y}$. Russell's conventions for reading abstracts with several variables at *21, such as $a\{\phi!(\hat{y}, \hat{x})\}b. = .\phi!(b, a)\ Df$, while resolving some such ambiguities, are incomplete by virtue of ignoring expressions with abstracts.

logic do not need to be reduplicated in each type, which would have made the connectives typically ambiguous. A connective like $\equiv$ or $\sim$ would have to be repeated in each type because it would flank propositions of different types. In *10 axioms are assumed which allow propositional connectives to apply directly to propositions of higher orders, and so be ambiguous. The project of *9 will only work, however, if every formula can be reduced to such a prenex form involving lowest order formulas. Perhaps Russell and Whitehead were unsure of this assumption, and so included both *9 and *10 in the final version.

The second interpretive issue concerning predicative functions in PM arises from the statement of the theory of types in *12. *12 repeats most notions from the introduction, including the problematic claim that all functions can be derived from matrices by generalizing over predicative functions. What differs from the introduction is the account of what functions are predicative. First the similarities in definitions ([PM], 161):

> Propositions which contain no apparent variables we call *elementary propositions*, and the terms of such propositions, other than functions, we call *individuals*.

and

> Let us give the name of *matrix* to any function, of however many variables, which does not involve any apparent variables. Then any possible function other than a matrix is derived from a matrix by means of generalization ...

but then we have:

> Let us denote by "$\phi\hat{x}$" or "$\phi(\hat{x}, \hat{y})$", or etc. an elementary function whose argument or arguments are individual. We will call such a function a *predicative function of an individual*. Such functions, together with those derived from them by generalization, will be called *first-order functions*.

Thus predicative functions are just the matrices, while first order functions in general include those derived by generalization over some of the individual variables. This is different from the account of predicative functions in the introduction.

At PM (164) this definition of predicative functions is repeated:

> A function is said to be *predicative* when it is a matrix. ... The fact that a function is predicative is indicated, as above, by a note of exclamation after the functional letter.

Chihara ([1973], 22) describes the difference in this way: "In *12, we are told that predicative functions are matrices, that is, not all first order propositional functions would be predicative! In contradistinction to this, we are told in the introduction that predicative functions of individuals are those that take individuals as arguments and that contain no bound variables that range over propositional functions."

Is there a simple way of characterizing this difference? The issue is what Russell means by a predicative propositional function and whether including a quantifier ranging over individuals affects the type of a propositional function of individuals of type $(\iota)/ \ldots$. Consider a proposition quantifying over all the people in a room. It presupposes the totality of those people. But a definite description using such a proposition doesn't presuppose them. The question, therefore, is not about which formulas are well formed, but rather, which types should be assigned in a comprehension principle to functions which depend on different totalities.

The instance of the comprehension principle guaranteeing the existence of the propositional function:

$(\hat{x}$ is the tallest person in the room).

is:

(1) $(\exists f^{(\iota)/1})(\forall x^{\iota})\{f(x) \equiv (\forall y^{\iota})[InRoom(y) \supset Tallas(x,y)]\}$

Compare this with:

(2) $(\exists f^{(\iota)/1})(\forall x^{\iota})\{f(x) \equiv InRoom(x)]\}$

That yields the propositional function $(\hat{x}$ is in the room). Both are predicative functions; only the latter is a matrix. It is true that (1) might seem to presuppose the totality of people while (2) does not, because of the quantifer ranging over all individuals y in (1). The following seems most in keeping with the introduction to PM, however. The propositional function $(\hat{x}$ is in the room) presupposes all its values, and since those have as constituents all the arguments, the function presupposes all its arguments, i.e., all individuals. But those individuals are the very things quantified over by both functions, hence both should be of the same type after all. On the other hand, if one thinks that quantifiers are themselves constituents of propositions and so of propositional functions, then it would seem that (1) and (2) should yield propositional functions of different types.

Thus apparently contradictory accounts of predicative and first order functions can be resolved if we see Russell as wavering over whether a quantifier which refers to "all" individuals has some dependencies additional to those of a simple function, which can be true of "any" individual. In PoM he certainly distinguishes the former as referring to a "class as one", while the latter only to the "class as many". If there is an additional dependency, then he is right to distinguish arbitrary first order functions from a special class that does not depend on the totality of individuals. While keeping a distinction between "matrices" and "predicative functions" is a way we might record such a dependency, Russell does it by distinguishing predicative from other first order functions.

This distinction between first order functions depending on whether or not they contain quantifiers over objects is likely what Russell is alluding to by saying that the theory of types in *12 is more "strict" than that in the introduction. Allowing only matrices to be predicative functions restricts the class of predicative functions. This account also makes the use of the symbol '!' uniform. In the introduction first order functions will be of the lowest order compatible with their arguments, and as such '!' will apply to them. In *12, where matrices are distinguished from other first order functions, only the matrices will be of the lowest possible order, and so deserve the '!'. It is his view about what counts as the lowest possible order that changes, not the definition of '!' as the symbol for such predicative functions.

At issue in resolving the character of predicative functions is how finely individuated the classification of types should be, beyond the discriminations absolutely needed to solve the paradoxes. The issue does not have real substance until the theory is combined with an axiom of reducibility that guarantees the existence of a coextensive predicative function for any other function. A more "strict" notion of predicative function will make that axiom more powerful, or at least change its force. As we will see below, however, the interpretation of the axiom of reducibility does not depend on this point about the definition of predicative functions, either. While seemingly an inconsistency, this is ultimately a minor issue that does not challenge the coherence of PM.

5.3 LOGICAL FORM AND LOGICAL TYPE

The third issue about the "authentic" system of types, over the relation between logical type and logical form, arises from the differences between the two developments of predicate logic in *9 and *10.

The relationship between types and logical form emerges in *9, where further distinctions of type seem called for:

> *9·131 *Definition of "being of the same type."* The following is a step-by-step definition, the definition for higher types presupposing that for lower types. We say that u and v are "of the same type" if (1) both are individuals, (2) both are elementary functions taking arguments of the same type, (3) u is a function and v its negation, (4) u is $\phi\hat{x}$ or $\psi\hat{x}$, and v is $\phi\hat{x} \vee \psi\hat{x}$, where $\phi\hat{x}$ and $\psi\hat{x}$ are elementary functions or (5)

u is $(y).\phi(\hat{x}, y)$ and v is $(z).\psi(\hat{x}, z)$ where $\phi(\hat{x}, \hat{y})$ and $\psi(\hat{x}, \hat{y})$ are of the same type, (6) both are elementary propositions, (7) u is a proposition and v is $\sim u$, or (8) u is $(x).\phi x$ and v is $(y).\psi y$, where $\phi \hat{x}$ and $\psi \hat{x}$ are of the same type.

It seems that while disjunctions will be of the type of their disjuncts, as will a formula and its negation, the argument structure and quantificational form of a function is relevant to its type. ∗9·131 seems to require that if two two-place propositional functions are of different types, then the result of binding the same variable in each will result in one-place propositional functions of different types.[10] As a result, the division of types would be finer than the system of r-types indicates. Propositions $(\forall x)Fx$ and $(\forall x)(\forall y)Rxy$, distinct on this account, are the same r-type, namely ( ). The r-type of a function also does not indicate the logical form of the arguments that it takes. For example, a function C of a single type $((\iota)/1)/1$ might take two different functions $F\hat{x}$ and $R\hat{x}b$ as arguments. In section ∗9·131 Russell seems to be considering the idea that functions of arguments with different logical forms ought to be of different types.

Yet what is the type of a proposition supposed to indicate? At one extreme it might simply sort formulas so as to avoid violations of the vicious circle principle that would lead to self predication or paradoxes using impredicative definitions. I have argued that it is also meant to record some features of the logical form of a proposition, namely the chains of dependencies on various totalities that are uncovered in the analysis of the constituents of a propositional function. The passages in ∗9 seem to suggest that the type of a function will indicate even more – namely, the structure of its arguments. Why should that be a relevant feature of a function? One project in ∗9 is to define connectives applied to a quantified formula in terms of quantified formulas including those connectives applied to matrices, as in:

$$∗9·03 \ (x).\phi x. \lor .p := .(x).\phi x \lor p \quad Df$$

This assumes that quantified formulas are crucially different from each other depending on the number of quantifiers involved. There is then a connection between the project of ∗9 and the seemingly strict notion of types occuring there. Russell certainly holds that the type of a function determines its range of significance, in the sense of the range of arguments to which it meaningfully applies. This is clear in:

∗9·14. If "ϕx" is significant, then if x is of the same type as a, "ϕa" is significant, and vice versa. Pp

---

[10]See the discussion in Chihara ([1973], 22–23).

and in ∗10 the related:

> ∗10·121 if "ϕx" is significant, then if a is of the same type as x, "ϕa" is significant, and vice versa. [∗9·14]

It follows from this proposition that two arguments to the same function must be of the same type; for if x and a are arguments to $\phi \hat{x}$, "ϕx" and "ϕa" are significant, and therefore x and a are of the same type. Later analytic philosophers seized on the role of types in determining the range of "significance" of a propositional function as a source of their notion of "category mistake" or "meaningless" assertion.[11] For Russell, however, it is more accurate to take the talk of "significance" as describing simply what arguments a function can take, and thus as describing the dependencies of propositions on propositional functions and arguments. Reading talk of "meaninglessness" as only expressing violations of type also provides a response to those who find some deep incoherence in the very attempt to talk about the theory of types in general. PM is not doomed to incoherence by somehow violating its own strictures on types in its very generalizations about types. Propositions about all types might be in violation of type theory and so meaningless in this technical sense, but not in the more general sense of being nonsense.

To return to our earlier example, are $F\hat{x}$, $R\hat{x}b$ and $(\forall y)R\hat{x}y$ of the same type? Through most of PM and according to the system of r-types, they are of the same type. But it is possible to see why Russell could waver on this point, and in ∗9 think differently. What if a proposition's meaningfulness is determined by the structure of the fact involving universals and particulars that it purportedly asserts? A proposition involving a function $C^{((\iota)/1)/1}$, say that expressing ($\hat{x}$ is a color), would seem only to apply to monadic propositional functions, those expressing color universals. '$C(F)$' would say that F is a color. But the function $R\hat{x}b$, which is the logical form of something like '$\hat{x}$ is the same color as b', just doesn't seem to fit. If 'b' is a name for the sky, this expression analyzes 'skycolored', a plausible expression for a color. But then there will be a proposition $C(R\hat{x}b)$, namely that being sky-colored is a color. What might be the structure of the fact that such a proposition describes? It would have to be that C can be involved in facts of differing complexities, one involving just C and F as consitutents, another with C, R and b, a metaphysical impossibility. This consequence is not a con-

---

[11]Ryle [1979] lists this as one of Russell's four significant contributions to philosophical methodology. (The three others are the use of logical analysis to reduce ontological commitment, the use of humor to deflate opposing views, and the deliberate formulation of tests or recalcitrant phenomena by which to judge his own theories.)

clusive *reductio* of the view, however. Russell holds exactly this position with regard to the relation of "belief" in his "multiple relation" theory. Russell could hold both that the type of a function must represent the analysis of the function into universals and particulars, and must also use the coarser grained account of r-types, but would do so at the cost of holding that almost all functions of functions behave like "belief" in being really of many different adicities, really "multiple" relations.

The most natural account, however, sees Russell as identifying the types of functions, such as $F\hat{x}$, $R\hat{x}b$ and $(\forall y)R\hat{x}y$, and so of abandoning the identification of types and logical forms. Somehow, even though the facts would be of different sorts, a single function could apply to arguments of all those different forms. To this extent, then, the language of PM will not be "logically perfect", it will not reveal the full analysis of the propositions which occur in it, but only enough of their structure for certain purposes.[12] The account just proposed does acknowledge that there is some tension between Russell's account of propositions in the multiple relation theory, and the account of propositional functions in PM. That tension, however, explains at least some of Russell's vacillation about types, in particular the pressure behind the move in $*9$ to distinguish types as finely as logical forms. Russell had a choice, on the one hand, of working out the consequences of having almost every relation really a "multiple" relation of various adicities, or in some other way explaining how a number of facts of very different seeming sorts could all be significant, or on the other, of giving up the assertion that the type of a proposition provides an exhaustive description of its range of significance.

---

[12] I agree then with a certain reading of Cocchiarella's claim ([1980], 108) that "... whereas the propositional functions that occur in a judgment are indeed 'fragmented' in the sense of analysis, nevertheless each propositional function, as well as the 'fragments' of that function that result upon analysis, retains its status in the judgment as a single entity." It is true that the propositional functions will be units in the symbolism of PM; however, upon ultimate analysis they will be 'fragmented' into talk about universals and particulars. Propositional functions, then, are no more in the ultimate ontology of PM than are propositions.

6

THE AXIOM OF REDUCIBILITY

It is often thought that Logicism was a failure, because when it avoided the Scylla of contradiction in Frege's system, in Russell's hands it fell into the Charybdis of requiring obviously nonlogical principles.[1] The axiom of reducibility is cited, along with the axiom of infinity and the axiom of choice, as another nonlogical principle which Russell had to add to his system in order to develop mathematics.

In this chapter I consider several questions about this criticism of the axiom. Why is it thought that the axiom of reducibility is not a principle of logic? What reasons does Russell actually give for doubting its logical status? Are they good reasons? The conclusion will examine the metaphysical status of predicative propositional functions and the axiom.

As we have seen, the ramified theory of types of the first edition of PM goes beyond the "simple" theory with its divisions between individuals, first-order propositional functions which apply to individuals, second-order propositional functions which apply to first-order functions, etc. It further subdivides each of these types according to the range of the bound variables used in the definition of each propositional function. In Russell's example the function ($\hat{x}$ has all of the properties of a great general) will itself be a property of great generals, but not one within the range of that particular quantifier "all". It will thus define a propositional function of a higher order than any of the variables bound by that quantifier. Similarly a difference of type would have to be marked in the theory of real numbers between the property "belonging to the set X" and "being the least upper bound of the set X", as the latter is defined in terms of a quantifier ranging over all members of X. Since numbers are defined as classes, and those in turn are defined in terms

---

[1] I borrow this image from Carnap ([1931], 41), who says that a successful logicism must avoid the Scylla of the axiom of reducibility and the Charybdis of the allocation of numbers to different orders.

of propositional functions, numbers will inherit the order distinctions of functions. The consequent division of numbers into different orders makes much ordinary reasoning seem invalid. The axiom of reducibility eases this difficulty. It asserts that for any propositional function, of whatever type, there is a coextensive propositional function of the lowest type compatible with its arguments, called a "predicative" propositional function:

$$*12\cdot1 \quad \vdash: (\exists f):(\phi x \,.\, \equiv_x .\, f!x)$$

In modern notation, using r-types and allowing for the general case of n-place predicates, we have:

$$(\exists f^{(\beta_1,\ldots,\beta_n)/1})(\forall x_1)\ldots(\forall x_n)[\phi(x_1,\ldots,x_n) \equiv f(x_1,\ldots,x_n)]$$

where $\beta_1,\ldots,\beta_n$ are the r-types of $x_1,\ldots,x_n$, respectively.

There will be a propositional function true of just those individuals with all the properties that make for a great general, which itself is of the same type as those properties quantified by "all". There will be a propositional function true of the least upper bound of a set X of the same type as the function "is a member of X", and so on. The instance of the axiom expressing the claim that there is a predicative propositional function coextensive with '$\hat{x}$ has all the properties of a great general' would be:

$$(\exists h^{(\iota)/1})((\forall x^\iota)\{[(\forall f^{(\iota)/1})Q^{((\iota)/1)/1}f \supset fx] \equiv h!x\})$$

This differs from an instance of the comprehension principle, which would only assert the existence of a non-predicative function h of type $(\iota)/2$.[2]

The ready availability of predicative propositional functions guaranteed by the axiom of reducibility allows those predicative functions to substitute for classes in Russell's famous "no-class" theory of classes. Sentences seemingly about "the class of fs" are to be analyzed as existential sentences asserting that some predicative propositional function coextensive with f has the given properties. The axiom of reducibility thus both avoids some of the stringency of the ramified theory of types and guarantees the existence of the predicative propositional functions that replace classes. It is these very virtues that have been the source of doubt about the axiom.

---

[2]Landini [1996] says that the axiom of reducibility just *is* Russell's comprehension principle, and that only predicative functions are values of variables in PM, unlike my more standard interpretation of the principle. More of his account below.

6.1   OBJECTIONS TO THE AXIOM

Objections to the axiom of reducibility combine several related points, in particular, that it makes an existence claim that is not purely logical, that it seems *ad hoc* and so lacks the obviousness of genuine logical principles, and finally, that the whole ramified theory of types of which it is a part is itself not purely logical, and, indeed, borders on incoherence since it seems to take back with the axiom all of the ramification of types, which is its hallmark. I consider these objections in turn.

It is often suggested that the axiom of reducibility is like the axiom of infinity in making an existence claim, and as such is not a principle of logic. Viewed as a comprehension schema the axiom looks like the axiom of separation from Zermelo-Fraenkel set theory. ZF, however, is seen as a rival to logicism as a foundational scheme.[3] Set theory is for those who have given up the project of reducing mathematics to logic, and instead resort to just postulating the existence of those basic, but distinctively mathematical, entities that are needed to develop the rest of mathematics. The axiom of reducibility also seems to postulate the existence of peculiarly mathematical entities, predicative propositional functions, and so would seem to be of a piece with set theory.

Russell himself was suspicious of a priori existence proofs. He does say that logic cannot prove the existence of certain things, such as God, or how many things there are in the world. But this is not a very good reason to say that logicism with the axiom of reducibility is a failure. One knows that no logicist program could possibly work if the problem lies in simply proving existence assertions from logic. In arithmetic we can prove many existence claims, for example, there is an even number between 4 and 8. Since arithmetic can prove an existence claim, if logicism were correct, then logic would imply an existence claim, which is impossible, Q.E.D. There is no need to find the particular source of the existence claim to disqualify the logicist program, we know the existence claim, though possibly hidden, must be there from the start.[4] (One might provide an analysis of mathematical existence claims that gives them some other logical form, just as Russell's theory of descriptions analyzes descriptions as not genuine singular terms. For Frege and Russell, however, there were legitimately logical objects, whether courses of values or propositional functions, and quantification over mathematical

---

[3] Gödel says that in the realist, simple theory which ought to replace the ramified theory of types, "... place of the axiom of reducibility is now taken by the axiom of classes, Zermelo's Aussonderungsaxiom ..." ([1944], 140–141).

[4] It has in fact been an important discovery to find out where an existence claim shows up in a development of mathematics, sometimes in a seemingly analytic truth as in a principle of abstraction for properties or in Frege's notorious Law V.

objects was to be reduced to quantification over them.) Surely then, it is no objection to the status of the axiom of reducibility as part of a logicist program to simply point out that it asserts an existence claim. The objection must rely on the nature of the existence claim which is made. One might argue that logic should make no assumptions about the number of individuals, i.e., lowest level entities, that there are. While one might want to avoid a free logic, and assume that the universe is not empty, the assumption of a countable infinity of objects, as made by the axiom of infinity, might lie outside of purely logical principles. As merely a claim about the existence of certain propositional functions, however, this restriction does not bar the axiom of reducibility from belonging to logic.

Another related objection is that adopting the axiom simply undoes the construction of the hierarchy of propositional functions that is the very purpose of ramifying the theory of types.[5] If the higher order classes of a given simple type are seen as constructed from those of lower order, then adopting the axiom of reducibility would be self-defeating. If all the classes there are have already been constructed at the first level, then all the convoluted ways of producing defining conditions for classes out of simpler classes do not really accomplish anything. Doesn't this redundancy make the constructions pointless? Quine argues that the axiom is a platonistic existence claim and so violates the only possible, constructivist, motivation for the ramifying the theory of types in the first place. Quine's objection thus combines the two lines of criticism I am discussing. He charges that the axiom both undoes the effect of the ramification and commits the theory to a platonistic view of propositional functions (which, when Russell's use/mention confusions are cleared up, amounts simply to a theory of sets).

Other criticisms of the axiom are more indirect. Following Ramsey, it is often charged that the ramified theory of types involves an unnecessary complication of the simple theory of types, one introduced in order to deal with the semantic paradoxes that are not properly logical paradoxes.[6] The axiom of reducibility then inherits the non logical character of the system to which it belongs. Accordingly, a defence of the axiom will require a defence of the ramified theory of types itself as a system of logic. The answer to these objections comes in seeing the ramified theory of types as a system of intensional logic which includes the "no-class" account of sets, and indeed the whole development of mathematics, as

---

[5] Quine ([1963], 249–258) presents this objection. See also Myhill, cited below, for a response.

[6] See Ramsey's ([1965], 1–61) *The Foundations of Mathematics.* See the discussion above in chapter 4.

just a part. A defence of the axiom of reducibility, then, leads to a defence of the whole ramified theory of types and the logicist project to which it belongs.

6.2 THE ORIGIN OF THE AXIOM

Although this chapter is concerned with the justification of the axiom of reducibility within Russell's views at the time of writing PM and after, a look at the earlier history of the principle will help to explain its role in his thinking. A casual account of the evolution of Russell's thought is that he first had a simple theory of types, designed to handle his original paradox of sets, later adding the "ramification" in order to handle the semantic paradoxes. Then, realizing that the ramification made impossible the project of reducing mathematics to logic, he introduced the axiom, undoing the effect of the ramification.

This account is inaccurate. It may follow the natural ordering of topics in a presentation of the theory of types, which Russell himself uses, but it does not present the historical development of the theory. To begin with, type theory was effectively ramified from its earliest formulations around 1906–1907, even when it was proposed in conjunction with the "substitutional" account and so was not properly an axiom about propositional functions, but rather propositions.[7] The distinctive feature of ramification is to distinguish propositional functions which take arguments of the same type by the ranges of the bound or "apparent" variables that occur in them. As the emerging story of the various attempts at solving the paradoxes has made clear, Russell did try to avoid a type theory. This was in part due to his desire to maintain the doctrine of the unrestricted variable, which was in turn due to the belief in the universal character of logic.[8] But once Russell accepted Poincaré's analysis of the paradoxes as due to a vicious circle, he immediately saw that the range of the universal quantifiers in propositional functions needs to be restricted to a specific totality; in other words, he saw the need for ramification.

Just before finally accepting the need for types Russell considered the "substitutional" theory of propositional functions. According to this theory the primitive quantifier ranging over both objects and proposi-

---

[7]Leonard Linsky has persuaded me that my attempt at revisionist history might be misleading. He has long maintained that the essence of the simple theory of types is present in Appendix B to *Principles of Mathematics*, and that the intensional, but not semantic, paradox of propositions in the last paragraph of that appendix requires ramification of the simple theory. (See above §4.2). I rather see the suggestions in the appendices to PoM as just sketches that were not full-fledged "theories". Even so, on that account, the theory of types did not remain unramified for long, and the ramification was justified by what seem to be logical rather than semantic paradoxes.

[8]See Hylton ([1980], 1–31)

tions is unrestricted, but the defined quantifier that seemingly ranges over propositional functions is restricted. This is not a real restriction of quantifiers, however, because expressions for propositional functions are "incomplete symbols" which can be eliminated by contextual definitions. The real range of quantifiers is all objects and all propositions. The next stage of development for Russell was to see the need for type distinctions among propositions. With OI (190–214), Russell adopts the vicious circle principle as the analysis of the paradoxes and the consequent need for at least type distinctions among propositions, while still denying the reality of propositional functions with his "substitutional" view. Yet he immediately acknowledges that "every statement containing x and an apparent variable is equivalent, for all values of x, to some statement fx containing no apparent variable" ([OI], 212). Thus, for example, propositions about all propositions of a given sort, say all those asserted by Epimenides, must be (materially) equivalent to some proposition which does not include such quantification. This claim amounts to an axiom of reducibility.

Poincaré thought that his vicious circle principle was incompatible with the logicist account of mathematical induction. Russell's paper, OI, includes a response to Poincaré on this issue. For a logicist, the principle of induction says that all properties possessed by 0 and hereditary with respect to the successor relation are possessed by all numbers. The vicious circle principle requires that the quantification over "all" properties must be restricted to avoid reference to any impredicative properties defined with apparent variables ranging over all numbers.[9] As this sort of quantification is required in so many uses of the induction principle, adopting the vicious circle principle seems to "destroy many pieces of ordinary mathematical reasoning" ([OI], 211). Thus Russell saw that the adoption of type theory with the consequent restriction of bound variables to ranges of significance undercuts those principles which seem to rely on unrestricted quantification (even when the real quantifiers are only those ranging over objects and propositions, as in the "substitutional" account). The definition of identity, that x and y are identical if and only if they share all properties, is another such example, and will be discussed more below.

This simultaneous appearance of types and an axiom of reducibility is all the more remarkable for the fact that at the time Russell did not even see the hierarchy of types as one of properties or propositional functions, but rather as simply of propositions. In OI he was still in the grip of the

---

[9]Poincaré would seemingly ban all impredicative properties, while Russell would restrict them to a distinct type.

"substitutional" theory, which attempted to define away propositional functions with contextual definitions and the primitive notion of replacing one object by another in a proposition. The axiom of reducibility, then, did not make its first appearance as a view about the existence of propositional functions, but rather as a necessity, given the need to restrict quantifiers to types. Given that restriction, generalizations over all properties must be replaceable by quantifiers ranging over only a certain type of properties.

The axiom of reducibility guarantees that restricting attention to properties of only one type will not invalidate standard patterns of reasoning about all properties, because if any property does not apply to an object, one of that chosen type will not apply to that object. Thus the induction principle says that any property possessed by 0 and hereditary with respect to the successor relation will be possessed by all numbers. The axiom of reducibility implies that any property of numbers will be coextensive with a predicative property. If a number lacks a property it will lack a coextensive predicative property, and if it has a property it will have a coextensive predicative property. Consequently Russell is able to use as his definition of identity the weaker claim that $x = y$ if and only if x and y have all the same predicative properties:[10]

$$*13 \cdot 01 \quad x = y. = : (\phi) : \phi! \, x. \supset . \phi! y \quad Df$$

The axiom of reducibility allows one to restrict attention to the predicative properties of x and y. A justification of the axiom of reducibility, then, must consist of a reason to believe that one can so restrict attention to the properties of one preferred type, the predicative functions.

In what follows I wish to explain the role of the axiom in Russell's thinking at the time of *Principia Mathematica*, when his ontology was considerably different. In fact the particular ontology he had in the background of PM is the source of the justification for the axiom at that time. What can be learned from its earlier appearance, however, is that the axiom was an integral part of the notion of a theory of types, not some afterthought used to patch up a defect resulting from the addition of ramification to an earlier, simpler theory of types. It is the whole ramified theory of types with reducibility that needs justification, not the axiom on its own.

6.3 DOUBTS ABOUT THE AXIOM

Let us turn, then, to Russell's views in PM. To evaluate those it is instructive to look at his reasons for the later abandonment of the axiom

---

[10]The more familiar version with a biconditional is proved directly as *13·11.

of reducibility, one of the characteristic differences between the systems of the first and second editions of PM. What reasons did Russell himself give for doubting that the axiom is logical? There is very little about it in the introduction to the second edition. All he says is:

> One point in regard to which improvement is obviously desirable is the axiom of reducibility (*12·1·11). This axiom has a purely pragmatic justification: it leads to the desired results, and to no others. But clearly it is not the sort of axiom with which we can rest content. ([PM], xiv)

Russell's objection is hardly explicit. We know what the objection amounts to by looking at the argument for the axiom in the introduction to the first edition:

> That the axiom of reducibility is self-evident is a proposition which can hardly be maintained. But in fact self-evidence is never more than a part of the reason for accepting an axiom, and is never indispensible. The reason for accepting an axiom, as for accepting any other propositions, is always largely inductive, namely that many propositions which are nearly indubitable can be deduced from it, and that no equally plausible way is known by which these propositions could be true if the axiom were false, and nothing which is probably false can be deduced from it. ([PM], 59)

He goes on to say that the inductive evidence for the axiom is good, so the real problem is that:

> ... although it seems very improbable that the axiom should turn out to be false, it is by no means improbable that it should be found to be deducible from some other more fundamental and more evident axiom. It is possible that the use of the vicious-circle principle, as embodied in the above hierarchy of types, is more drastic than it need be, and that by a less drastic use the necessity for the axiom might be avoided. ([PM], 59–60)

In the second edition Russell says that by following Wittgenstein's example in making the logic extensional one can avoid the axiom but still "prove many useful theorems".[11] So this objection is that the axiom should be proved from other more self-evident axioms, or avoided in the proof of the desired theorems by adopting some different axiom.

---

[11] Russell even claims this about the theory of types in the first edition, claiming that the principle of induction could be derived without the axiom of reducibility. This claim is shown incorrect in John Myhill [1974].

Russell then does not require that the axiom of reducibility be self-evident, and does not express any doubt about its truth; rather he thinks it is redundant. (It is important to note that Russell includes logical axioms among those that need not be self-evident, as long as they have the right deductive strength.) At the time of the first edition he thought that the axiom might be redundant because an excessively strong form of the vicious circle principle had introduced too many types, which then had to be integrated with the axiom of reducibility. The vicious circle principle denies the existence of any entity, such as a totality or propositional function, which depends on itself in the wrong way. If a propositional function depends on a totality, then it cannot be a member of that totality, and hence belongs to a new type, thus the ramification of type theory. With the principle of extensionality anything true of one propositional function will be true of every coextensive one, so the only thing on which a propositional function can depend is its extension, and so the type theory will not be so extensively ramified. A function may be identified by the functions used to define it, but that really means only on the extensions of the functions used to define it.[12] Extensionality thus weakens the force of the vicious circle principle by limiting what a propositional function can depend on, and thus what it could depend on viciously. Other principles limiting the dependence of propositional functions by identifying some which are distinguished in the full ramified theory would have the same effect. It is clear that even at the time of writing the introduction to the second edition of PM, Russell thought the principle of extensionality was stronger than necessary. Thus this doubt about the axiom of reducibility was a doubt about the vicious circle principle and the number of type distinctions it introduces, rather than a doubt about the existence claim made by the axiom.

A richer guide to Russell's thinking about the axiom of reducibility is in the *Introduction to Mathematical Philosophy*, written in 1918, between the two editions of PM. There he again expresses doubts about whether the axiom has the character of a regular principle of logic. One worry is that the axiom is not general or widely enough applicable. Thus: "This axiom, like the multiplicative axiom and the axiom of infinity, is necessary for certain results, but not for the bare existence of logical reasoning" ([IMP], 191). He goes on to explain that it does not have the universal applicability of, for example, the quantifier laws, and so could be just added as a special hypothesis whenever it is used. Here, obviously, Russell is concentrating on the use of the axiom of reducibility

---

[12]Hatcher's system of types, discussed in §4.3 above may in fact more accurately represent the type theory in the second edition of PM.

in the construction of the natural and real numbers. It is not so clear that the axiom would seldom be used outside the theory of classes and mathematics, as can be seen from its role in proofs about identity. The need for impredicative definitions in mathematics, in particular for the notion of the least upper bound of a set of real numbers, has led many to see the "certain results" to which Russell alludes as only a limited part of higher mathematics. Indeed, the appeal of developing a "predicative" analysis has suggested that the axiom is in fact debatable. Of course Russell's project was primarily to develop mathematics and so his attention was focussed precisely on the role of impredicative definitions in mathematics. Attention to the identity of indiscernibles should remind us of the frequency of talk about all properties of a thing within logical theory and metaphysics. Since without the axiom of reducibility such talk is banned, we see that the axiom is not solely needed for the development of higher mathematics, such as analysis.

Russell goes on to question the necessary truth of the axiom of reducibility, demanding that a logical truth be true in "all possible worlds" and not just in this "higgledy-piggledy job-lot of a world in which chance has imprisoned us" ([IMP], 192). So Russell has qualms about both the generality of the axiom and its necessary truth, features he takes to be characteristic of logical truths. These remarks are most likely the source of many claims that the axiom of reducibility is not a principle of logic because it is not intuitively obvious enough, or a general enough principle of reasoning.

Russell's objections here are a mixed lot and do not directly bear on the issue of whether or not the axiom is a principle of logic. He has a theoretician's concern that the axiom is *ad hoc* and could be replaced by more basic principles. He is also concerned that the axiom is not a necessary truth, but that feature does not distinguish logic from a very general metaphysical theory of the world. Russell's concern that the axiom is only of use in mathematics, and not a general principle of reasoning is similar in this regard. Given Russell's earlier remarks that axioms need not be directly evident, it is hard to attribute to him a view of logic which is distinct from a more substantive metaphysical theory, other than by differences of degree.

These, then, were Russell's various qualms about the axiom of reducibility. What can be said in defence of the axiom? Should Russell have had such qualms about it, given its role in his logic?

6.4 *Principia Mathematica* AS INTENSIONAL LOGIC

The axiom of reducibility plays a crucial role in the logic of PM because of the distinctive role of predicative propositional functions in that system. It is the realist view about propositional functions, in particular, a view about predicative propositional functions as encapsulating the real features of objects, which serves as a justification for the axiom within the philosophical system of PM.

First it is important to clarify the role of the axiom of reducibility in Russell's theory of classes. It does not just undo the effects of the ramification as the "constructivist" reading suggests. For what follows I rely on the recent work of Alonzo Church and Leonard Linsky on what might be called the "intensional interpretation" of *Principia Mathematica*.[13] They have argued that despite the central project in PM of developing mathematics, which is an extensional subject, the logic of PM is fundamentally intensional. It is not even that PM is only devoted to the extensional portion of what might be a broader intensional logic; the intensional nature of the logic in PM explains many otherwise puzzling features of its presentation. One example is the role of scope in the theory of definite descriptions. In extensional contexts the scope differences do not have any logical effect, as long as the descriptions are proper. Proper definite descriptions can be treated like proper names with regard to logical operations like substitution and quantification. Why, then, are scope indications introduced with such care, if not because it is expected that many contexts will be intentional? Likewise several features of the "no-class" theory also depend on the intensionality of propositional functions. Russell says that the axiom of reducibility is the key to his no-class theory of classes. Linsky's interpretation of this claim goes like this: Russell's contextual analysis of classes, the "no-class" theory, is very similar to the analysis of definite descriptions, including the possibility of scope distinctions. The basis of the theory of descriptions is:

$$*14\cdot01 \quad [(\imath x)(\phi x)].\psi(\imath x)(\phi x). \; = \; : (\exists b) : \phi x. \; \equiv_x .x = b : \psi b \quad Df$$

This is the substance of Russell's theory from [OD] that 'The ϕ is ψ' amounts to 'There is exactly one thing b that is ϕ and it is ψ. The initial part of the formula in brackets indicates the *scope* of the description $(\imath x)(\phi x)$, namely, that ψ is the context from which the description is to be eliminated. In cases like Russell's "The present King of France is not bald", there will be different choices of context for the description; "... is bald" or "not ... is bald", depending on what ψ is taken to be. The first reading requires that there be a unique King of France and

---

[13]See Church [1976], L. Linsky ([1983], Appendix), and Goldfarb [1989].

that he be not bald, the second allows either that there is not a unique King of France, or if there is, that he is not bald. The description is considered "proper" if there is exactly one such ϕ. The no-class theory likewise eliminates class expressions $\hat{z}(\psi z)$ from contexts f in which they occur:

$$*20 \cdot 01 \quad f\{\hat{z}(\psi z)\}. =: (\exists \phi) : \phi! x. \equiv_x .\psi x : f\{\phi! \hat{z}\} \quad Df$$

This can be read as saying that the class of ψs is f just in case there is a predicative function ϕ that is co-extensive with ψ and that ϕ is f. Unlike the theory of descriptions, the no-class theory is not presented with any corresponding indicators of the scope of the class abstracts. They could easily be added, however[14]. Then just as it is true (and proved in PM $*14 \cdot 3$) that scope distinctions for (proper) definite descriptions make no difference in extensional contexts, it is true that scope distinctions make no difference in extensional contexts for class expressions.[15] That this fact *could* be easily expressed and proved shows that the logic was set up to handle intensional contexts.

There are two conditions to be met for descriptions such as "the F" to behave like names with regard to scope and substitution. It is not only necessary that one restrict oneself to extensional contexts, but also that the description be proper. A similar requirement for class abstracts to behave like names is that, in addition to occurring in extensional contexts, the requisite predicative propositional function must exist. But the latter is precisely what the axiom of reducibility guarantees. It guarantees the existence of the predicative function ϕ that is coextensive with the given ψ. So, Linsky's argument goes, the fact that Russell ignored scope distinctions for class abstracts, while he explicitly marked them with descriptions, shows that he saw himself as restricting his talk of classes to talk of extensional mathematical contexts, but not so restricting the full logic of PM. The axiom of reducibility was still essential for the no-class theory. It provides the correlate of the assumption that a description is proper, the existence assumption that is essential for establishing that class abstracts can be treated like names of classes, and not as sensitive to scope distinctions.

Given the particular contextual definition of class expressions that Russell presents, the axiom plays a crucial role in the theory of classes.

---

[14]The notion of scope in conjunction with class abstracts is mentioned at the very end of the introduction ([PM], 84).

[15]As claimed at PM (180). Gregory Landini ([1998], 166–167) points out that the principle analagous to $*14 \cdot 3$ would require not only that f be truth-functional but also that χ be extensional and only then is it the case that $f\{[\hat{x}(\phi x)].\chi \hat{x}(\phi x)\}. \equiv .[\hat{x}(\phi x)]f\{\chi \hat{x}(\phi x)\}$. For definite descriptions the corresponding principle holds even if χ is intensional.

While having the force of a comprehension principle, it does not assert
the existence of some new, non-logical category of entity, but rather just
of a predicative propositional function coextensive with an arbitrary
propositional function. The axiom of reducibility, then, does not just
undo the ramification of the theory of types. It is crucial in the reduction
of classes to logic, and unless one assumes that logicism is false and that
any talk of classes is not part of logic, it seems to be a quite legitimate
logical notion for Russell – provided, of course, that a claim about the
existence of a predicative propositional function with a given extension
can be seen as a logical principle.

What, then, of the charge that the axiom of reducibility undoes the
whole point of the hierarchy of types of propositional functions? That
charge assumes that the only point of the hierarchy of types is to represent the possible constructions of propositional functions and hence
of classes. What view could hold, rather, that all the classes have been
constructed at the level of predicative functions? The answer is that
propositional functions of higher types are needed to capture intensional phenomena. The predicative functions are needed to reconstruct
the extensional part of logic, that part which deals with the extensions
of predicates, or classes. The higher types are needed for intensional
phenomena, cases where the same class is picked out by distinct propositional functions. This view requires seeing the ramified hierarchy of
PM not as a constructivist hierarchy of classes but rather as a theory
of propositional functions which includes as a part the theory of classes,
but which does much more. Of course predicative propositional functions are not extensional. They can be distinct yet coextensive. Rather,
all extensional talk about classes is analyzed as a general (existential)
claim about predicative propositional functions.

What then is so special about predicative propositional functions that
one can adopt a "comprehension" principle asserting the existence of a
coextensive predicative propositional function for every arbitrary propositional function? I return to this question after the following digression.

6.5   GRELLING'S PARADOX AND THE AXIOM

Attention to the intensional nature of propositional functions is crucial
for understanding the response to one further objection to the axiom of
reducibility. This line of objection originates with Leon Chwistek, and
is reformulated by Copi [1972].[16] For the formulation of the problem

---

[16]See Leon Chwistek, "Antinomies of Formal Logic" ([1921], 338–345), who
presents it as a version of Richard's paradox.

and the reply I follow Myhill [1979].[17] The suspicion is that the axiom either lets some semantic paradoxes back in, or only allows them to be blocked with implausible assumptions. To formulate Grelling's paradox we are asked to formulate a somewhat artificial property of linguistic expressions, in particular, of predicates. A predicate is '*heterological*' if it does not possess the property it expresses. Thus 'short' as a linguistic item, is short (only five letters in one syllable) and so is *not* heterological. By those standards of length, 'long' is not long and so is heterological. The paradox arises when we ask whether the predicate 'heterological' is heterological. If it is, then it does not possess the property it expresses and so is not heterological. If not, then it does not possess the property of being heterological that it expresses and so is heterological, a contradiction.

To formalize the argument leading to the paradox we need a two place relation between expressions and the properties (propositional functions) they designate: $D(x, f)$. The special propositional function of being heterological can then be defined:

(1) $(\forall x)\{Het(x) \equiv (\exists f)[D(x, f) \wedge \sim f(x)]\}$

We also need enough assumptions about the D relation to establish that $Het(\hat{x})$ has a name 'h', in the sense that the following can be derived:

(2) $(\forall f)[D(h, f) \equiv (f = Het(\hat{x}))]$

(Variations in the technical analysis of this argument hinge on the details of what sort of systems, like Gödel numbering, can be developed in the theory of types, and then what sort of disquotation principles relating mentioned and used expressions are provable.[18])

Now for the argument leading to the paradox. We suppose $Het(h)$. By the definition of $Het(\hat{x})$ at (1):

(3) $(\exists f)[D(h, f) \wedge \sim f(h)]$

Consider a particular such f, say f_0,

(4) $D(h, f_0) \wedge \sim f_0(h)$

But then it follows by (2) that:

(5) $(f_0 = Het(\hat{x})) \wedge \sim f_0(h)$

so

(6) $\sim Het(h)$

---

[17]There are several other discussions of the objection and this reply in Chihara [1973], Hazen ([1983], 371–374) which is informal and relates the problem to other issues in logic and Church [1976], which provides full technical details.

[18]See Hazen [1983].

Suppose, on the other hand, that (6) is true. Since then

(7) $D(h, Het(\hat{x}))$

it follows that:

(8) $(\exists f)[D(h, f) \wedge \sim f(h)]$

and so

(9) $Het(h)$

'Heterological' both is and isn't heterological, a contradiction.

The resolution of Grelling's paradox in the ramified theory of types is immediate when the defined propositional function $Het(\hat{x})$, the designation relation D and the quantifier in (2) are assigned r-types. Suppose we assign types as follows in the definition (1):

(1') $(\forall x^{\iota})\{Het^{(\iota)/2}(x) \equiv (\exists f^{(\iota)/1})[D^{(\iota,(\iota)/1)/1}(x, f) \wedge \sim f(x)]\}$

then the corresponding assignment in:

(2') $(\forall f^{(\iota)/1})[D^{(\iota,(\iota)/1)/1}(h, f) \equiv (f = Het^{(\iota)/2}(\hat{x}))]$

is not even well formed because f and $Het(\hat{x})$ are of different r-types. The vicious circle principle docs not allow $Het(\hat{x})$ to be defined in terms of a totality of propositional functions of which it is a member, and so the system of types blocks the definition. When other assignments of types are tried, the contradiction is no longer derivable. The variable f in (2) must range over $Het(\hat{x})$ for the argument to work, but if the types in the definition (1) of $Het(\hat{x})$ are observed, ie. if it must be of a higher order than the functions to which it applies, then the arguments that h satisfies $Het\hat{x}$ and that it doesn't both fail.

The worry about the axiom of reducibility comes from the fact that while $Het(\hat{x})$ must be of a type, say $(\iota)/2$, if it expresses a property of functions of type $(\iota)/1$, there will none the less be a *coextensive* function $Het^*(\hat{x})$ which is of that lower type. By the axiom of reducibility:

$(\exists f^{(\iota)/1})(\forall x^{\iota})[fx \equiv Het^{(\iota)/2}(x)]$

Call it $Het^*(\hat{x})$. It follows then that:

(1") $(\forall x^{\iota})\{Het^{*(\iota)/1}(x) \equiv (\exists f^{(\iota)/1})[D^{(\iota,(\iota)/1)/1}(x, f) \wedge \sim f(x)]\}$

Suppose that there is an h^* which designates $Het^*(\hat{x})$. We have:

(2") $(\forall f^{(\iota)/1})[D^{(\iota,(\iota)/1)/1}(h^*, f) \equiv (f = Het^{*(\iota)/1}(\hat{x}))]$

Suppose $Het^*(h^*)$, then:

(3") $(\exists f^{(\iota)/1})[D^{(\iota,(\iota)/1)/1}(h^*, f) \wedge \sim f(h^*)]$

Consider the particular instance f_1:

(4") $D(h^*, f_1) \wedge \sim f_1(h^*)$

Then it follows by (2″) that:

(5″) $(f_1 = Het^*(\hat{x})) \wedge \sim f_1(h^*)$

(6″) $\sim Het^*(h^*)$

But then $Het^*(h^*)$ so again the contradiction follows for Het^*.

Has the axiom of reducibility reinstituted the very paradox that the ramification of types eliminated? Not so, argues Myhill. The paradox is rather a *reductio ad absurdum* of the assumption that there is an h^* which designates $Het^*(\hat{x})$. We must conclude that $Het^*(\hat{x})$ is not nameable. Unlike $Het(\hat{x})$, which is expressed by a formula and clearly nameable, $Het^*(\hat{x})$ is only known to exist as an instance of an existential quantifier. As one might expect, and as Church [1976] has worked out in great detail, there is a connection between this analysis of Grelling's paradox and Tarski's solution of the "semantic" paradoxes in terms of a hierarchy of meta-languages. Any system of names for propositional functions will fall short in expressive power, even though that shortcoming can easily be rectified in another language, which in turn will have a shortcoming, etc.

This account of the resolution of the paradox reveals several aspects of propositional functions. That they are not all nameable (in a given language) reinforces their image as extra-linguistic entities. As well, two distinct but coextensive propositional functions can differ enormously, one nameable and the other not. An axiom of extensionality identifying coextensive propositional functions would reinstate the contradiction and so require a different solution, as would simply adopting the simple theory of types. Both these approaches, however, can take the argument as the proof that 'heterological' does not pick out the intended propositional function, thus solving the paradox only at the cost of losing the ability to represent intensional notions.

6.6   THE IDENTITY OF INDISCERNIBLES

The distinctive character of predicative propositional functions can be seen in the details of Russell's charge that the axiom of reducibility is not a necessary truth. Russell says that:

> The axiom, we may observe, is a generalized form of Leibniz's identity of indiscernibles. Leibniz assumed, as a logical principle, that two different subjects must differ as to predicates. Now predicates are only some among what we call "predicative functions", which will include also relations to given terms, and various properties not to be reckoned as predicates. Thus Leibniz's assumption is a much stricter and narrower one than ours. ([IMP], 192)

Russell goes on to say that the axiom seems true of the actual world, for:

> ...there seems to be no way of doubting its empirical truth as regards particulars, owing to spatio-temporal differentia- tions: no two particulars have exactly the same spatial and temporal relations to all other particulars. But this is, as it were, an accident, a fact about the world in which we happen to find ourselves. ([IMP], 192)

How is the axiom of reducibility a "form" of the identity of indis- cernibles? The most general version of the principle of the identity of indiscernibles says that $x = y$ just in case all the same predicates (prop- ositional functions) apply to x and y. Leibniz's version is much stricter, requiring that distinct objects differ by some monadic (atomic) pred- icate, i.e., by some universal. The axiom of reducibility allows one to steer a middle course, by giving the force of the most general principle by only requiring that identicals share all the same predicative proposi- tional functions. Suppose that ϕx but not ϕy where ϕ is not predicative. Then, according to the axiom, there is a predicative propositional func- tion f coextensive with ϕ, and thus true of x, which distinguishes x from y with predicative functions alone. Accordingly, Russell's definition of identity:

$$*13\cdot01 \quad x = y. = : (\phi) : \phi!x . \supset . \phi!y \quad Df$$

$*13\cdot01$ is this "restricted" form of the identity of indiscernibles, and the above reasoning is equivalent to the proof of the theorem:

$$*13\cdot101 \quad \vdash : x = y . \supset . \psi x \supset \psi y$$

one "half" of the more familiar identity of indiscernibles. (The more controversial half of the principle, that if x and y have all the same properties, then $x = y$, follows immediately from the fact that if they share all properties, they share all predicative properties, and, by def- inition $*13\cdot01$, are identical.) The axiom of reducibility is possibly a stronger principle than is needed to prove the identity of indiscernibles from the definition of identity, for the proof only requires that objects sharing all predicative properties share all properties in any given type, whereas the axiom of reducibility accomplishes this result by providing a predicative property which is coextensive for each arbitrary property. This may have been one of the points where Russell suspected that the axiom of reducibility might be replaced by a simpler principle. Still, how- ever, he accepts the axiom to the extent of calling it a "generalized form" of the identity of indiscernibles. Reasons for accepting that generalized principle would then, for Russell at least, provide a justification for the axiom of reducibility.

What then is the reason for accepting the axiom of reducibility and its accompanying definition of identity? I believe that for Russell it was not just a matter of stipulation that made classes coincide with predicative propositional functions. Rather, he thought that predicative propositional functions really express the genuine universals and relational properties which individuate things in the world. Objects do not always differ in their monadic properties, as Russell argued against Leibniz. It was a distinctive feature of Russell's philosophy that he argued for the reality of relations and hence the irreducibility of some relational properties. Thus "being two miles from x" is a perfectly good relational property, not reducible to any monadic properties of x. Predicative functions comprise the original stock of one-place properties plus all the possible relational properties, and then the Boolean combinations of all of those.[19] For individuals these are the properties represented by matrices.[20]

It is because Russell saw predicative propositional functions as expressing more than just monadic qualities that he speaks of the axiom as a "generalized" version of Leibniz's principle. Leibniz, according to Russell's account, would presumably endorse an even stronger "axiom of reducibility" to the effect that every propositional function is equivalent (by analysis and not just coextensiveness) with some conjunction of monadic qualities.

Russell feared that it might be a matter of arbitrary postulation, or in any case only contingently true, that the predicative propositional functions should suffice to distinguish all objects. Why shouldn't some higher type property allow us to distinguish objects? Russell considers examples like "having all the qualities of a great general" and "being a typical F" (where the latter seems to mean something like having all the properties shared by most Fs). The answer can be seen in the very nature of these examples. Higher type propositional functions do not really introduce new properties of things. They may characterize new ways of thinking of or classifying them, but they do not introduce any new real universals.

---

[19]Hazen ([1983], 367–368) points out that the axiom seems to require that there are predicative propositional functions to pick out any arbitrary class of objects, including those that are infinite. Predicative functions thus range beyond anything that could be considered a "concept". He is considering a conceptualist reading of the axiom, but even on the realist reading I am proposing it is hard to argue that any arbitrary class of objects share some "nature", even if one of a highly derivative sort. The axiom thus seems to make a highly contentious metaphysical claim.

[20]With the proviso that if there are general facts about objects, represented by formulas including also quantifiers over individuals, that more than just matrices will be predicative. See §5.2 above.

If one grants that Russell had in mind some distinction between propositional functions and universals that have a metaphysically important role as that which underlies the real qualities of things, then it is clear that predicative propositional functions inherit some of the character of universals. One need not argue that any two objects will be distinguished by some universal that one has and the other lacks. That would be to claim that all objects have a unique nature, an implausible metaphysical assumption. But one might hold that something accounts for the particularity of objects, if not their qualities or natures, then perhaps their locations. If one holds a relational view of space, then the view that spatio-temporal location individuates particulars is one which allows a relation to individuate.[21] If one were only interested in individuating objects two at a time then universals or relational properties might be sufficient. One could say of objects with different natures that one has F and the other does not, where F is a universal in the nature of the one object. For objects with the same nature one could use relational properties as one does with spatio-temporal relations of concrete particulars. When whole classes of objects are involved one may require Boolean combinations of universals as well as relational properties. Some of the objects may be distinguished by being F, others by being G, others by not being H, and so on, so that the predicative propositional function "being F and G but not H ... " is needed to mark off the class. (If the account of predicative functions in *12 of PM is followed, then every predicative function will simply be such a matrix built up from "elementary" functions which will express universals.) Russell's qualms about the axiom of reducibility being contingent thus amount to the worry that such a scheme of spatio-temporal relations and properties is merely a contingent characteristic of the world.[22]

As I have presented it, the axiom of reducibility marks out the special role of predicative propositional functions as the properties which individuate things in the world. One still needs the whole ramified hierarchy of propositional functions to handle all the things that can be said of the world, or thought of it, including the whole realm of intensional

---

[21]See Armstrong ([1978], chapter 11) for a discussion of spatio-temporal location and particularity.

[22]Hazen ([1983], 364) points out that if *minds* are among the individuals in the world, and they are individuated by their thoughts, then higher order properties will be needed to individuate real individuals. However, by the "multiple relation" theory, beliefs will in fact be first order relational properties, involving individuals and universals as relata. As noted above, Hazen also points out that the arbitrary classes of objects will need a common "nature", something clearly not defensible on a conceptualist account, and still at least questionable on the sort of realist account I am proposing.

phenomena.[23] This account makes the axiom of reducibility out to be a
metaphysical principle. It is one of great generality, however, certainly
unlike any principle about numbers as abstract entities or of the sort
that might occur in any special science. Still, this way of viewing the
axiom helps to account for Russell's qualms. Though the axiom states a
very general principle of metaphysics, does it really have the necessity
required of a principle of logic? Is it logically necessary? Russell was
not sure. Ultimately it was the lure of doing without the full ramified
theory by adopting the principle of extensionality that made him give
up the axiom. But giving up on intensional phenomena was an extreme
solution. It undid the whole relation between classes and propositional
functions that was at the heart of the first edition of PM.

The axiom of reducibility was an integral part of the theory of types.
From the beginning it was clear that if a theory of types requires restricting the ranges of bound variables to a given range of significance,
or type, then those principles which seem to require quantifying over
all properties must be stronger than necessary. Identity, while seeming
to require the sharing of all properties, really only requires the sharing
of properties of the lowest, predicative order. Similarly,the existence of
sets, which should allow a set for all predicates, really only requires sets
for all predicative properties. In addition, all numbers and properties
of numbers to which the induction principle will apply are clearly represented at the lowest type. Some criticisms of the axiom and its role
seem to require forgetting the intensional nature of the logic, and hence
the use for all those additional, non predicative propositional functions.
Russell was aware of the need for an independent justification for the
principle, one that showed how conclusions about numbers, classes and
identity could be settled by only considering predicative propositional
functions. That predicative propositional functions are all that is needed
for the theory of classes and numbers follows directly from the "no-class"
theory and the definition of numbers as classes. The adequacy of predicative propositional functions for the definition of identity and other
more "metaphysical" or non-mathematical applications of the logic of
PM comes from the distinction between propositional functions and universals, and what is close to a match between predicative propositional
functions and universals. Predicative propositional functions mark the
real kinds in the world. That this is so, is a fairly substantive metaphysical claim about the world, and so is not obviously of the same generality

---

[23] As Hazen [1983] points out, if there are mental entities that do not supervene
on physical objects, and so might be individuated by their mental properties such as
the propositions they entertain, not all objects will be individuated by predicative
functions.

or as clearly "necessary" as the other principles of Russell's logic. It was, however, also not obviously out of place in the metaphysical logic of *Principia Mathematica*.

7

LOGICAL CONSTRUCTIONS

In "Logical Atomism", from 1924, Russell describes the "heuristic maxim" that guided his work: "Whenever possible, substitute constructions out of known entities for inferences to unknown entities" ([LA], 161). Earlier, in the *Introduction to Mathematical Philosophy*, he says:

> The method of "postulating" what we want has many advantages; they are the same as the advantages of theft over honest toil. Let us leave them to others and proceed with our honest toil. ([IMP], 71.)

What is this honest toil of construction? In particular, what is its role in Russell's metaphysics? Encouraged by differing things that Russell says about his many examples of constructions, the project has been interpreted variously as nominalist ontological reduction, philosophical analysis of ordinary notions, explication in precise terms of vague ordinary concepts, or as an anticipation of mathematical constructivism. That Russell's project was in fact a confused amalgam was the thrust of criticisms beginning in the 1930s with L. Susan Stebbing [1930] and, famously, by John Wisdom [1931] in *Mind*. Their criticisms seem to have taken hold, and although some new aspects of constructions have come into prominence since then, the overall assessment that Russell's project was confused has become the accepted view.

Rather than as a mess of confusion the project of "logical construction" should be seen as a collection of related proposals, having a common source and similar goals. The source is in the original logicist analysis of numbers as classes of equinumerous classes. Then followed the analysis of definite descriptions in 1905, later the "no-classes" account of classes and finally, by 1918, an account of matter as constructed. In this chapter I will present some of the history of criticisms of Russell's notion and then turn to the constructions one by one to point out the common thread and defend the coherence of the various projects. These constructions, and in particular the theory of definite descriptions, are

110

the subjects of large bodies of literature. I do not propose to present a systematic account of them all, providing a simple guiding principle for them all. Rather, the focus in each case will be on the metaphysical implications of the construction, on the ontological status of constructed entities, and the role of the notion of dependency that underlies the theory of types.

To begin, there seems to be a use/mention confusion, or at least sloppiness, in speaking of things as indifferently "logical constructions", "incomplete symbols", and "logical fictions" when it is the expressions for constructions that are the symbols.[1] What's more, to say that something is a "fiction" seems to deny it existence, unlike calling it a "construction", which would seem to be a real thing, even if something that is made of something else. To start sorting out these expressions, then, we must identify the symbols as "incomplete" and what they purport to name as the constructions or fictions.[2]

Stebbing found two aspects of constructions that are further sources of confusion, using the construction of matter as an illustration. On one hand, material objects are classes of sense data, and so are of a different logical type from sense data. On the other hand, however, Russell does compare logical constructions and entities known only inferentially, "by description", as somehow correlative. Constructions were provided to replace the material entities that are inferred from experience rather than directly observed. In this sense the construction is the same logical type but differs in epistemological status. Russell suggests that he is replacing inferred entities with constructions. Second, Stebbing saw more confusion in the claim that it is ordinary talk of physical objects that is subject to constructions. A problematic theoretical notion such as "matter" might be given an analysis in the sense that hitherto obscure language could be replaced with precise substitutes. The claim that a table is a construction is not of that sort, however. It requires a wholesale shift of language about physical objects, not just the occasional analysis. Both Wisdom and Stebbing proposed that the most useful notion of construction should be defined in contrast with the notion of logically proper names, which they both preferred to represent with the notion of object in Wittgenstein's picture theory of meaning in the *Tractatus*

---

[1]In PM both the "... phrase which expresses a proposition" (44) and definite descriptions (66) are called "incomplete symbols". *Classes* are called "incomplete symbols" at PM (84). In IMP (182) we find "... classes are in fact, like descriptions, logical fictions, or (as we say) 'incomplete symbols'." Consider also: "... you can construct a logical fiction having the same formal properties ... " ([PLA], 23) and a few pages later: "And I and the chair are both logical fictions, both being in fact a series of classes of particulars ... " ([PLA], 241).

[2]This point is already made in Wisdom [1930].

Logico-Philosophicus [1922]. "Incomplete symbols" are then identified as those expression not analysed into names in the (pictorial) logical form of a sentence.

Contrary to the widespread acceptance of these early charges that Russell confused several different distinctions, I hope to identify some elements common to his various constructions and to reconcile these clearly different aspects of the notion of logical construction. Stebbing's criticisms are useful, however, for their identification of important issues to be addressed in providing an adequate account of Russell's project. Understanding the nature of the meaningfulness and ontological import of incomplete symbols, the contrast between hypothesis and construction, and the extent to which constructions provide an *analysis* of ordinary notions, will all be important for an adequate understanding of the nature of logical constructions.

Discussions of logical constructions did not end with Stebbing and Wisdom's criticisms. The connection between logical constructions and incomplete symbols has been a focus of some attention in more recent discussions of the theory of definite descriptions and the ontology of the theory of types. Many of Russell's own remarks encourage the notion that logical construction is primarily a tool for the project of nominalist reduction, allowing one to show that some purported entity is nothing but a linguistic mirage.[3] Russell repeatedly refers to constructed entities as "logical fictions" and suggests that they are not really objects at all. He calls the expressions for those constructs "incomplete symbols", that is, not really constituents of propositions. This use of terminology seems to go even one step beyond nominalism by denying that expressions for constructions are even (mere) names. These remarks suggest the commonly held view that the idea of logical construction is the very the origin of linguistic analysis, where analysis is seen as a project of avoiding the metaphysical urge to reify language, and indeed most other philosophical errors, through careful analysis of language. This nominalist reading of Russell's ontology has influenced recent discussions of the theory of types, in particular the discussion of Russell's views on propositional functions. A second issue of current interest is the role of the notion of an incomplete symbol in the theory of "On Denoting" and its relation to current notions of constituents in "logical form". Russell seems to hold that incomplete symbols such as definite descriptions (and other quantifier expressions) are not really constituents of proposi-

---

[3]The primary site is in Russell himself in MPD, as was discussed in chapter 1. J.O. Urmson ([1956], 30) concludes that "to show that 'X' is an incomplete symbol is tantamount to showing that there are no Xs'". See also the exchange between Perkins and Urmson in *Analysis* (Perkins [1972], Urmson [1973], and Perkins [1974]).

tions, and that there is thus a gulf between the apparent form of many sentences and their proper logical form.

Russell's thinking about constructions was dominated by the first and most important example of it in his logical and mathematical work, the construction of numbers as equivalence classes of equinumerous classes. As time went on, he added different sorts of logical projects to the category of constructions, all of them sharing the essential elements, but differing with regard to some of the questions raised above. Constructions are not all philosophical analyses, ontological reductions, proposals for regimentation of ordinary notions for specific purposes, though elements of these all appear in some constructions. If anything, a construction should primarily be seen as a *replacement* for an ordinary notion. That replacement does provide an explicit notion where the original may have been imprecise, but it can have very different logical and epistemological properties from the original. In particular, a construction has precise, provable features where the original is vague or leads to skepticism. Underlying all examples of construction, however, are questions of logic and ontology. Each construction Russell proposes has definite ontological significance, which this chapter purposes to explore. However great the role of epistemological issues in Russell's philosophy, it is primarily his logical ontology that was the focus of his notion of logical form and logical construction.

Russell's own accounts of constructions support the idea that they developed out of the construction of numbers. In LA (160–164) Russell lists his logical constructions:

(1) The principle of "abstraction" – substituting equivalence classes for a common quality, eg. a shared magnitude. A "very important" example is Frege's construction of the natural numbers as a class of similar sets.

(2) Elimination of classes as "single entities" by the methods of PM∗20.

(3) Definite descriptions.

(4) Mathematical examples; series, ordinal numbers, and real numbers.

(5) Points and instants as sets of events of finite duration and extent.

(6) Matter constructed from events.

The inclusion of the theory of descriptions and the no-class theory in this enumeration shows that constructions are not simply restricted to entities that might be seen as classes of other entities.[4] The inclusion

---

[4] *cf.* Sainsbury [1980] for a contrary view that constructions are all classes and that classes are to be in turn eliminated in terms of propositional functions by the no-

of contextual definitions among constructions shows that, if anything, we should say that it is *talk* about certain entities that is constructed rather than the entities, or even names for the entities. That is not to say that the expressions are constructed; rather that construction is a logical tool providing definitions of certain expressions seemingly about certain entities, but in fact dependent on others. In addition, I have maintained above that Russell held propositions to be constructions according to the multiple relation theory of judgment, and propositional functions in turn to be constructions out of propositions, although he does not, and indeed could not, present the construction as a formal definition.

A common goal of these constructions, which can be found in Frege's construction of the numbers and on through all the later examples, is presented in the paragraph leading up to the statement of the maxim:

> One very important heuristic maxim which Dr. Whitehead and I found, by experience, to be applicable in mathematical logic, and have since applied to various other fields, is a form of Occam's Razor. When some set of supposed entities has neat logical properties, it turns out, in a great many instances, that the supposed entities can be replaced by purely logical structures composed of entities which have not such neat properties. In that case, interpreting a body of propositions hitherto believed to be about the supposed entities, we can substitute the logical structures without altering any of the detail of the body of propositions in question.This is an economy, because entities with neat logical properties are always inferred, and if the propositions in which they occur can be interpreted without making this inference, the ground for the inference fails, and our body of propositions is secured against the need of a doubtful step. The principle may be stated in the form: 'Whenever possible, substitute constructions out of known entities for inferences to unknown entities'. ([LA], 160–161)

The definition of numbers as equivalence classes was a crucial step in Frege and Russell's logicist project. The goal of that project was to show that mathematics does not rely on intuition in Kant's sense, because mathematical truths can be reduced to logical truths via a series of definitions. Through the work of Bolzano, Dedekind and Peano, it was clear that real analysis could be reduced to the theories of of classes and of natural numbers as axiomatized in Peano's postulates. The problem

---

classes theory, and those in turn are to be seen as just predicates via a substitutional interpretation of the higher order quantifiers of PM.

was then to find definitions of the primitive notions of Peano's theory, number, successor and 0, in terms of logical notions so that the postulates could then be derived by logic alone. What Russell describes as the method of "postulation" would be to rest content with Peano's axioms, taking them as postulating the existence of numbers with certain properties. Rather, Frege and Russell thought, those "neat" properties of numbers which are described by the axioms ought to be *derivable*, given only the proper definitions of numerical notions. In this case a construction is simply a definition provided with certain goals in mind, namely, the reconstruction of certain "neat" features of some purported entity that are derivable from some prior theory.[5] The Frege/Russell construction does provide an ontological reduction of numbers to classes, a way of avoiding an extra postulated entity in terms of other objects. It is not a nominalist reduction, however, one which might replace commitment to numbers with mere names or numerals. The ontological commitments of arithmetic remain after the reduction. The claim that there is a number greater than 3 but less than 5 will be provable from the complete theory as before, as well as the "external" assertion that there are numbers. Frege quite obviously saw classes as objects, and Russell carries over the analysis in its entirety. Some other constructions, in particular the theory of descriptions, do not provide a reduction, but the use of definitions in providing proofs of "neat" properties is the common model for all.

7.1 DEFINITE DESCRIPTIONS

The theory of descriptions is often presented as accomplishing an ontological goal. Indeed it is often seen as the very model of how to avoid unwanted ontological commitments. In "On Denoting" Russell does present his own theory as superior to Meinong's account, with its golden mountains and round squares. That Russell's account avoids commitment to a present king of France seems to be one of the arguments he presents in its favor. But it has long been noted that denying that definite descriptions need to have a referent is not the essence of the theory. Think of "proper" definite descriptions such as 'the present queen of England'. A sentence of the form 'The F is G' is true if and only if there is one and only one F, and it is G. When such a sentence is true there will be an individual of the sort F (only one), and that individual will be G. To take our example, the theory of descriptions does not provide a reduction of monarchs to some other sort of thing. In particular it does not say that 'the F' is just a piece of language that does not stand for an in-

---

[5] Compare Carnap's [1931] similar account of constructions. He finds the discovery of derivations in formal systems to be the heart of the method.

dividual. It does, however, show that not *all* uses of definite descriptions carry with them some ontological commitment. Sentences including 'the present king of France' by themselves do not carry any ontological commitment to individuals. Sentences including 'the F' which are true (and in which the description has primary, or widest, scope) will, however, commit us to Fs.

Is this some new sort of ontological reduction, one that is partial, reducing the commitment of some sentences about objects but not others? In what way can that be seen as a *reduction*? The answer comes from standing the account of descriptions against the construction of numbers. The theory of descriptions is, first of all, formally a definition. In *Principia Mathematica* it is formulated as:

$$*14{\cdot}01 \quad [(\imath x)(\phi x)].\psi(\imath x)(\phi x). = : (\exists b) : \phi x. \equiv_x .x = b : \psi b \quad Df$$

The occurrence of the quantifer ranging over objects in the definiens shows that this is not a way of eliminating ontological commitment to individuals. The theory of descriptions does not avoid all ordinary ontological commitment. After all, true sentences using 'the present queen of England' with widest scope still commit us to the existence of the queen. What the theory of descriptions allows us to avoid is a commitment to logical objects, such as descriptive (or "denoting") concepts or things that can be deduced to exist from the mere logical form of a descriptive statement, regardless of its truth value. These would be objects required if a proposition is to be even meaningful, not only when it is to be true. Most philosophers have thought that one could only be so committed to objects as necessary for denoting phrases to be even meaningful by holding a referential ('Fido'–Fido) theory of meaning, viz., that the referent of a term was its meaning. But there are other reasons that objects might show up in a theory of meaning, and it was to reduce such use of objects that Russell adopted his theory of descriptions.

In keeping with the account of constructions quoted above, there are neat properties that this construction is meant to capture which can now be proved rather than simply postulated. Most important of these are that ways in which descriptions behave like proper names. For example, co-denoting descriptions may be substituted for each other. Thus, if the F is the G then the F is H if and only if the G is H[6]. This is proved in:

$$*14{\cdot}16 \quad \vdash : .(\imath x)(\phi x) = (\imath x)(\psi x). \supset : \chi\{(\imath x)(\phi x)\}. \equiv .\chi\{(\imath)(\psi x)\}$$

But descriptions also have logical structure. It should follow that if the

---

[6]Provided of course that the descriptions 'the F' and 'the G' have *wide* scope, and that is indeed the way the following theorem is to be read, given conventions about scope in PM.

F exists then *the* F is *an* F:

$*14\cdot22 \quad E! (\imath x)(\phi x). \equiv .\phi(\imath x)(\phi x)$

PM continues thus, through the whole of section $*14$. Another important consequence of Russell's analysis was noted above, that a *true* sentence involving a description (with wide scope) *does* have an ontological commitment. If a 'the F is G' is true there must be one (and only one) F. But the mere occurrence of a description in a sentence does not have that ontological commitment, which is how a sentence can contain the expression 'the present king of France' without committing us to any object. These are the logical or neat properties that descriptions have which Russell would like to be able to derive from logical principles, rather than having to assert them by postulate. That descriptions have these last logical features is in fact disputed; thus the tradition of Frege and Strawson, who insist that improper descriptions lead to truth value gaps. That these neat features are disputed does not show that Russell did not consider them advantages of his theory, however, or that the program does not assert that such consequences follow by logic from a construction. The existence of a dispute over the consequences of a construction should be taken as justification for the view that constructions are explications of ordinary concepts, regimentations intended to change ordinary concepts in order to make them logically precise. Russell, after all, does say that sentences with improper descriptions, such as 'The present King of France is bald' are "plainly false", which would surely be a neat property ([OD], 46).

Russell identifies logical constructions with incomplete symbols, and this talk of "symbols" does seem to support the notion that constructions provide a nominalist ontological reduction. I wish to argue to the contrary that Russell is indeed ontologically committed to some logical constructions, despite their expression by "incomplete symbols". What then is an incomplete symbol? The notion of definite descriptions as incomplete symbols appears in "On Denoting", though without the name:

> *Everything*, *nothing*, and *something* are not assumed to have any meaning in isolation, but a meaning is assigned to *every* proposition in which they occur. This is the principle of the theory of denoting I wish to advocate: that denoting phrases never have any meaning in themselves, but that every proposition in whose verbal expression they occur has a meaning. ([OD], 42)

The notion also occurs in *Principia Mathematica*, here in connection with propositions:

> Owing to the plurality of the objects of a single judgment, it follows that what we call a "proposition" (in the sense in which this is to be distinguished from the phrase expressing it) is not a single entity at all. That is to say, the phrase which expresses a proposition is what we call an "incomplete" symbol; it does not have meaning in itself, but requires some supplementation in order to acquire a complete meaning. ([PM], 44)

The notion appears straightforward; an incomplete symbol is not given a meaning by itself but rather only an account of the meaning of sentences in which it occurs.[7] The definition of definite descriptions is not an explicit definition in the sense of being an identity sentence or universally generalized biconditional with '$[(\imath x)(\phi x)]$' on one side of the identity or equivalence symbol. Instead we are shown how to "eliminate" the description from contexts in which it occurs. The positive account of how incomplete symbols do have meaning seems clear.

What, however, is the force of the negative claim that an incomplete symbol has no "meaning in itself"? There are two recent views on this matter, but, as I shall argue, both mistake the importance of this feature of the theory. The standard view is that not only are definite descriptions not primitive symbols of PM, but they are not properly seen as occuring in propositions in any way. On this view the moral of the comparison with *indefinite* descriptions is that the expression 'the F' is no more a part of a proposition than is 'All Fs'. The latter expression dissolves into analyses of different occurrences, as when 'All Fs are Gs' becomes '$(\forall x)(Fx \supset Gx)$' which is not of subject/predicate form. Similarly 'The F is G' becomes a quantified expression which has no single part corresponding to 'the F'. Russell himself had previously supposed that quantifier expressions did correspond with constituents, namely denoting concepts which, in the case of indefinite expressions would "ambiguously denote" individuals. Those individuals would not be constituents of the proposition. This account would explain how the theory of descriptions should be seen as an ontological reduction, namely, an elimination of denoting concepts. One might think of the expression '$[(\imath x)(\phi x)]$' as a name for a denoting concept, and thus the elimination of the name for the concept would lead to an ontological saving. The most distinctive feature of the theory, on this view, is that it avoids the commitment to denoting concepts by denying the correlation of surface

---

[7]Echoing Frege's maxim "never to ask for the meaning of a word in isolation, but only in the context of a proposition" ([1884], x). While Frege intended this principle to apply to all words, Russell clearly restricts it to only some.

linguistic form and logical form.[8] On this view the theory of descriptions achieves its goal by showing that what may look like a part of a sentence in surface form will disappear in logical form.

David Kaplan [1972] sides with this account of incomplete symbols, and it is in turn the basis of his criticism of the theory of descriptions. He identifies the essence of logical construction in the difference between syntactic form and logical form. It is the fact that definite descriptions are syntactically singular terms which disappear upon logical analysis that makes them incomplete. He proposes as an alternative a logical analysis that keeps definite descriptions as constituents of sentences and adds the "analysis" to the truth and denotation conditions. Thus the class of definite descriptions will be defined in the syntactic definition of *terms*, and clauses like the following will be added to the truth definition:

'$[(\imath x)(\phi x)]$' denotes the unique object which is ϕ if there is one

and for τ a singular term (including now definite descriptions)

'τ is bald' is true iff 'τ' denotes something which is bald.

Something will have to be said about what happens if a description τ doesn't denote, whether 'τ is bald' must be false or might be neither true nor false, but such will be the various different theories of descriptions. Kaplan thinks that it is essential to Russell's theory of descriptions that the truth conditions of sentences involving descriptions not follow nicely the apparent syntax of sentences with descriptions. It is precisely to the extent that there is a mismatch that descriptions must be considered incomplete symbols and so constructions.

The considerations above about constructions show why Russell would reject Kaplan's proposal. It is precisely those semantic features of definite descriptions, that they contribute to truth conditions what they do, that are the "neat" properties of descriptions. That a sentence with a description 'the F' is true just in case there is exactly one F, etc., ought to follow by *logic*, rather than by the additional postulation of certain neat properties. Statements about the contribution of a part of speech to the truth conditions of sentences in which it occurs would have to be seen as postulates in the meta-language, rather than logical consequences of definitions. What we see as a sort of analytic truth, the statements

---

[8]It has become clear that in fact much of the argument in "On Denoting" is primarily directed against Russell's own prior theory of denoting concepts, rather than against Frege or Meinong, as superficially appears to be the case. See Peter Hylton [1989]. Hylton insists, however, on the importance of the difference between logical analysis and linguistic form as the real significance of the theory of descriptions.

of a meta-language about truth conditions, do not appear as logical in Russell's logic.

Stephen Neale [1990] rejects Kaplan's account of incomplete symbols. He thinks that descriptions are constituents of the logical form of propositions, even on Russell's account. In the spirit of the earlier discussions of Stebbing and Wisdom, Neale claims that for Russell an incomplete symbol is simply one that does not directly refer. Thus anything other than a logically proper name or primitive predicate constant will be an incomplete symbol. Russell does say that to know what a proposition means one must be acquainted with its constituents. The singular terms that directly stand for those objects of acquaintance (and predicates that stand for universals) name the real constituents of propositions and everything else is an incomplete symbol. That, according to Neale, is why definite descriptions are incomplete symbols. As a result being incomplete is not incompatible with corresponding to a syntactic component of a sentence in a correct logical analysis. In fact, says Neale, the account of truth conditions that Kaplan offers as an alternative above is just another way of phrasing Russell's *own* theory. Neale himself presents a more sophisticated syntactic analysis, one in keeping with Government and Binding syntactic theory, but on the same general lines as Kaplan's proposal. He argues that definite descriptions are in fact noun phrases of the form of generalized quantifiers, rather than singular terms as Kaplan claims. Neale argues that there are tests for the syntactic distinction between singular terms and quantifiers and that they classify descriptions with quantifiers. A sentence that contains a description, 'The ϕ is ψ', which Russell presents as having the real logical form:

$$(\exists x)(\forall y)[(\phi y \equiv y = x) \ \& \ \psi x]$$

Neale says has a logical form more like:

[the x: ϕx] (x is ψ)

Kaplan says that it is the gap between the syntax of the original sentence and its real logical form that makes the description an incomplete symbol and makes any language with definite description operators logically imperfect. Neale argues that his proposed logical form is precisely the same as Russell's, just offered in a notation that was not available to Russell. For Neale this gap between apparent and real logical form is just an accidental feature of Russell's theory of descriptions, whereas for Kaplan it is essential.

On my account this debate misses the point of what it means to see definite descriptions as logical constructions. The issue is not whether definite descriptions belong to a syntactic category such as "singular term" or "quantifier" or rather cannot be identified with any syntactic portion of a sentence. The point is that definite descriptions have some logical import which must be derivable from a proper account, however descriptions are classified. PM gives a definition of contexts containing definite descriptions so that neat logical properties possessed by descriptions needed in the mathematical work of PM turn out to be derivable from *logical* features of the sentences superficially containing them. What Russell found was that the construction can go sentence by sentence. As long as there is a proper procedure for converting sentences one can construct the sentences as a whole rather than piece by piece.

There is also an ontological distinction between definite descriptions and at least one other quantifier, the universal quantifier. While the expression 'All Fs' is incomplete the component quantifier '∀' might well be seen as a constituent of a general proposition, a constituent which makes the difference between a conjunction of instances and a general fact. Similarly negation corresponds with the distinctive feature of negative facts. (Disjunction, on the other hand, while logically primitive is nowhere even hinted to correspond with some feature of facts.) One might then see a difference between the universal quantifier and other "generalized quantifiers" such as descriptions in that the latter do not directly involve genuine constituents of propositions. However, Russell does not seem sufficiently worried about finding the real primitive logical connectives to make this the sole substance of his claim that descriptions are incomplete symbols.[9] Still, the proposed analysis of descriptions in *14·01 may be seen as one that more clearly shows the structure of facts involving descriptions than an analysis which would treat the descriptions themselves as quantifiers.

Neale correctly points out that with a proper theory of generalized quantifiers one *could* construct sentences containing definite descriptions syntactic piece by piece. In claiming that his account is part of a general theory of natural language, Neale suggests that it should be an *analysis* of the meanings of ordinary language sentences that would produce the theory of descriptions, and not any regimenting construction. To the extent that logical constructions do not proceed according to the surface form of sentences they may be seen as not providing an analysis of

---

[9]While in the introduction to the Second Edition of PM, Russell does praise the discovery of the Sheffer stroke and proposes redoing the whole of PM with that connective as primitive, he does express doubts about whether "incompatibility" is a logically primitive notion that can replace negation in PLA (III), the discussion of negative facts. I think he saw the primitive connectives of PM as ontologically primitive, but was unsure whether that consideration alone should guide the choice of primitives. Hence the flirtation with the Sheffer stroke.

natural language, but rather as something more like a regimentation or proposal to improve on natural language. This is how the project of logical construction has traditionally come to be tied with that of proposing logically perfect languages, and the criticism of natural language has come to be seen as semantically defective. This feature of the theory, however, is incidental to the project, and is not its core.

Neale is wrong to simply identify incomplete symbols with expressions other than logically proper names and constants. The notion has positive content. An incomplete symbol will be one whose logical import, or neat features, can be captured in a contextual definition, or, in the case of propositions, is something that is to be treated as not standing for a distinct entity. The import of sentences containing incomplete symbols is to be captured with other sentences in which those symbols do not occur. Neale is right in supposing that when Russell denies that incomplete symbols have meaning in isolation, the contrast is between descriptions on the one hand and logically proper names and primitive logical symbols on the other. He is also right to say that it is not essential to Russell's thesis that no logical construction can be defined as the meaning of a syntactic constituent, such as the determiner or noun phrase of a sentence. For Russell, even the analysis of an atomic sentence Rab as expressing the value of an application of a propositional function $R\hat{x}b$ to an object a, would not be a real analysis in terms of constituents with which we are acquainted. The real constituents are the relation R and the two constituents a and b, all of which can be objects of acquaintance. Russell himself, then, would be able to see a sentence as the result of the application of certain functions to certain arguments, even when the function and argument are not ultimate referents of logically proper names. There is nothing in this notion of analysis, that would rule out an analysis of descriptions as generalized quantifiers, $i.e.$, second order propositional functions that apply to first order propositional functions. One must distinguish, however, between an analysis into ultimate constituents of a proposition with which one is acquainted, and the analysis of propostions into functions and arguments. The latter can give meaning to syntactic constituents such as noun and verb phrases but is not an ultimate analysis.[10]

----

[10]This sort of distinction is made by Michael Dummett ([1981], 65). He identifies the analysis of Rab into a and $R\hat{x}b$ as one that would be used to understand logical inferences, and the other into a, R and b, and the syntactic structure of the sentence, as the analysis appropriate to explaining the understanding of a sentence. It would seem, however, that definite descriptions, while not ultimate parts of the latter sort of analysis, could still be relevant units for understanding the meaning of whole sentences in which they occur.

7.2   THE MULTIPLE RELATION THEORY

Russell called what replaced his "Russellian" Propositions the "multiple relation theory" (usually, "... of belief" or "... of judgment"). While nominally an account of the attitudes of belief and judgment, the emphasis in the account is on eliminating the need for propositions as objects of a relation of belief or judgement. When explaining this account of propositions, Russell sometimes uses the language of the theory of definite descriptions, saying that symbols for propositions are "incomplete symbols" that are to be treated as only parts of larger expressions and not meaningful in their own right.[11]

This theory must not to be taken to say that propositions are really only sentences, as one might take a description to be "just a symbol", for Russell distinguishes the linguistic expression from the purported entity. Propositions are not linguistic items; rather, they are logical constructions. Russell does not provide the construction, as he does with descriptions or the no-class theory, nor is it clear how the construction would be accomplished. This suggests, however, that Russell saw the status of something as a construction as a genuine ontological fact, and the presentation of the construction as something to be searched for.

Despite the aggressive criticisms that the theory attracted from early on, the multiple relation theory of propositions is a natural extension of the notion of logical construction. It returns to the original model of equivalence classes, unlike the theory of descriptions ([IMP], 141). Consider the example of constructing colors on the basis of a similarity relation that Russell discusses in chapter IX of *The Problems of Philosophy* [1912]. One would replace the property or universal, say whiteness, with a class. That class would consist of all the objects bearing the appropriate relation of similarity to a paradigm white thing. Since the relation of similarity is an equivalence relation we can construct equivalence classes of objects bearing the relation to all others in their own class. The paradigm object in each class serves as a way of identifying or indexing the classes. Formally, when S is the similarity relation, and i a particular paradigm, the equivalence class will be $\{x : S(i, x)\}$. Notice that the monadic color property has been constructed with the use of a binary similarity relation. Now consider Russellian propositions, which

---

[11]Landini ([1993], 380 and, again, [1998], 288) says that they literally are definite descriptions, for example, 'The proposition that Desdemona loves Cassio is true' will be analyzed as 'The fact which corresponds with the state of some mind m understanding with respect to Desdemona, loving and Cassio, exists'. All talk of propositions will include such a description even if not a proper one, ie. if there is no such fact. This is a clever proposal, but seems to be one which would have been made explicitly if it were really Russell's intention.

we would represent as ordered sequences of objects and properties. The proposition that a and b stand in the relation R would be represented as a sequence, say $< R, a, b >$. A proposition involving a three place relation, that a, b, and c stand in the relation R_1, would be represented as a four element sequence: $< R_1, a, b, c >$, and so on.

Contemporary constructions are conducted within set theory, so all constructed entities are sets of other things. Some are constructed as sequences, but, via a construction of sequences as sets, ultimately all such constructions are done with sets. Russell, however, constructs classes using propositional functions, so classes are not available to construct propositions. Russell's own construction of propositions is exactly what one would expect if sequences are not available. Equivalence classes, as we saw above, are constructed with binary relations. A class of ordered pairs can be similarly constructed with a three place relation. Consider a class of simple propositions including one of the form $F(a)$, which we would represent as sequence $< F, a >$. The class can instead be constructed using a *three place* relation B, such that $< F, a >$ will be in the class just in case $B(i, F, a)$, where i is the index that picks out the class. The index allows one to group different propositions together, just as the paradigm index of color allows one to group different color classes together. Thus in one proposition class we may find $F(a)$, $R(a, b)$ or $S(a, b, c)$. These will be classed together by i in the relations $B(i, F, a)$, $B(i, R, a, b)$ and $B(i, S, a, b, c)$. This is, of course, precisely the multiple relation theory of belief. If the class of propositions is that which the individual i believes, then the B relations construct precisely those propositions. Now B will take various numbers of arguments, depending on the proposition believed, and will thus be multi-grade. Russell was familiar with this notion, and would include not only variations in the number of arguments of B but also variations in their type. 'B' is *typically ambiguous*, to be interpreted as of the appropriate type for the arguments to which it applies. If universals and particulars differ in type then there will be even more B relations, each corresponding to a possibly coherent combination of universals and particulars in a proposition. There would be less of an obvious "order problem", of the sort that seems to have been identified by Wittgenstein. This is the problem of explaining what it is that makes $B(i, R, a, b)$ possible, but not $B(i, a, b, R)$, or even $B(i, a, b, c)$. (As well, what is the difference between $B(i, R, a, b)$ and $B(i, R, b, a)$ and why does each one represent the belief that it does, *i.e.*, that it is a that bears R to b, rather than vice versa?) If the B relations only take certain series of typed arguments, corresponding to coherent propositions, it will be possible to see why there are only some of these beliefs and not others, but the problem may reappear in a less blatant form. Why then are there only some such B relations and not others? Which ones there are seems to be a logically contingent matter of the existence of certain universals, when the logical form of propositions would seem to be a logically necessary fact.

Russell soon developed qualms about this construction, most of which seem to revolve around these issues of order.[12] The objections in detail, however, seem to center on issues of how acquaintance and understanding, as epistemological relations, can involve notions of logical form, rather than doubts about the construction as metaphysically adequate.

What then is the ontological status of propositions? Propositions are indeed not "single entities". They are not postulated primitives of Russell's logic. Rather, they are constructed entities. Does the construction serve as a reduction? Russell does indeed avoid quantifiying over propositions in PM (with the notable exception of *14·3) usually allowing propositional variables to appear as "apparent" or free variables. This practice invites the intepretation of the symbols as really schematic letters. But Russell does not maintain that propositions are merely linguistic entities such as sentences. The phrase that *expresses* a proposition, he says, is an incomplete symbol, but the proposition is not an incomplete symbol or expression. Propositions are real, constructed entities, just as numbers are real, but constructed entities. The model here is the construction of numbers from classes rather than definite descriptions. It looks as though, in addition to sense data and other particulars, universals and facts in Russell's ontology, one must also add functions and propositions with some sort of existence, albeit of a derivative or secondary sort. He uses the language of "incomplete symbol" and "construction" when discussing them, but unlike the other examples cannot and indeed could not provide a definition, contextual or of any sort, of the logically basic symbols that represent them. The multiple relation theory proposes that assertions about propositions are dependent upon genuine facts involving belief and other attitude relations, subjects of those attitudes and the constitutents of the belief. But it does not provide a translation of assertions about propositions to assertions about those facts in the way that the no-class theory does translate talk about classes into assertions about propositional functions. Because there is no way to distinguish universals from functions, and facts from propositions in the language, there could be no way to provide such a reduction. Yet we are supposed to think of propositions as though they were a construction from those facts. The symbols for them are incomplete after all. In the introduction to the second edition of PM Russell says that with the

---

[12]See Griffin [1985].

introduction of extensionality "... classes, as distinct from functions, lose even that shadowy being that they retain in *20"([PM], xxxix). It appears that propositions and functions must also be granted a "shadowy" existence, enough to be quantified over and and so the values of variables and constants, without there being any analysis or elimination of such talk by definition. The realist ontology I have found in Russell's logic suggests that this existence should be seen as some sort of dependence or supervenience on the basic ontology of particulars, universals and facts. Here "logical" construction has metaphysical import.

Russell's theory of definite descriptions and his multiple relation theory have a particular connection with his epistemology which might suggest another interpretation of logical constructions and incomplete symbols.[13] Both in "On Denoting" and later, Russell connects the theory of descriptions with the epistemological distinction between knowledge by acquaintance and knowledge by description, via his "Russellian principle": "Thus in every proposition that we can apprehend (i.e., not only in those whose truth or falsehood we can judge of, but in all that we can think about), all the constituents are really entities with which we have immediate acquaintance" ([OD], 56). This might suggest that objects are to be constructed and so terms for them should be treated as incomplete symbols, just in case they are not possible objects of immediate acquaintance. Construction, then, would be a mental act, uniting objects of acquaintance in order to give us access to other objects with which we cannot be acquainted. Since there are no propositions to be acquainted with we rely on acts of judgment to tie together genuine objects of acquaintance. Construction would be an act of the mind necessary for thinking of objects indirectly or for tying together objects of thought. But this account does not fit with the actual use that Russell makes of constructions. To begin with, he sees the construction of matter as an *alternative* to his earlier account of knowledge. Matter is known by description as the cause of such and such sense data. It is not an account of how that indirect knowledge is achieved. He replaces the postulation of matter as a thing of which we have no "real" knowledge with the construction of matter from sense data. Furthermore, only some of the objects referred to by incomplete symbols are the sort of things that might be known only indirectly. Plausibly, if matter or other minds are the cause of sense data, they might only be known by description. But classes, numbers and propositions are not things known only indirectly. They are not objects with which we lack direct contact, but entities of

---

[13]This interpretation was urged on me by Robert Tully in his comments on an earlier version of this chapter.

a different kind altogether. Russell does restrict logically proper names to those things with which we can be acquainted. But it is as much a mistake, then, to see all other objects as constructions as it is to see all other expressions as incomplete symbols.

7.3 THE NO-CLASS THEORY

With the very different constructions of definite descriptions and propositional functions in mind, now consider the "no-class" theory of classes. On the surface the no-class theory looks much like the theory of descriptions. It takes a context '$f(\ldots)$' in which a class expression '$\hat{z}(\psi z)$' occurs, and provides a contextual definition in which the class term is replaced by quantifiers and bound variables ranging over propositional functions:

$$*20\!\cdot\!01 \quad f\{\hat{z}(\psi z)\}. =: (\exists\phi) : \phi!x. \equiv_x .\psi x : f\{\phi!\hat{z}\} \quad Df$$

(The class of ψs is f just in case there is a predicative function ϕ that is co-extensive with ψ and that ϕ is f.) This allows for the elimination of all class expressions in favor of expressions about functions. This principal definition is supplemented by:

$$*20\!\cdot\!02 \quad x\epsilon(\phi!\hat{z}). = .\phi!x \quad Df$$

which then eliminates the ϵ symbol which applies to functions after $*20\cdot$ 01 is used. Several other definitions analyse occurrences of bound class variables α, such as:

$$*20\!\cdot\!071 \quad (\exists\alpha).f\alpha. = .(\exists\phi).f\{\hat{z}(\phi!z)\} \quad Df$$

This is no more of a nominalist avoidance of ontological commitment than the theory of descriptions is. The theory of descriptions may eliminate apparent commitment to such entities as the present king of France, but certainly not to the present queen of England. The existential quantifier in the definiens of the latter ranges over individuals and the uniqueness clause identifies Elizabeth Windsor as the unique satisfier of the matrix of that quantifier. There will be, in general, no unique propositional function which bears the relation to a class that Elizabeth Windsor bears to 'the present queen of England'. While only one individual can be identical with "the F", there will be many predicative propositional functions equivalent to $\psi\hat{z}$.[14] On the other hand, there is more likely to be some propositional function or other which satisfies the function f, especially if f is a mathematical property which characterizes the extension of a function. There will, to that extent, be fewer non-denoting class

---

[14]The lack of a requirement of uniqueness has been seen as a difficulty for the no-class theory, one that almost leads to incoherence. For a discussion of Carnap's version of these objections, see L. Linsky [1987].

terms than non-denoting descriptions. Clearly, avoiding all ontological commitment to anything but referring expressions is not the aim of the no-class theory.

Perhaps, then, the theory should be viewed as a *reduction* of classes to propositional functions. We are, after all, allowed to quantify over only propositional functions in the end. Once more, however, the construction is aimed more at allowing the proof of certain desired theorems than at the reduction or elimination of ontological commitment.

> We have seen that an extensional function of a function may be regarded as a function of the class determined by the argument function, but that an intensional function cannot be so regarded. In order to obviate the necessity of giving different treatment to intensional and extensional functions of functions, we construct an extensional function derived from any function of a predicative function $\psi!\hat{z}$, and having the property of being equivalent to the function from which it is derived, provided this function is extensional, as well as the property of being significant (by the help of the systematic ambiguity of equivalence) with any argument $\phi\hat{z}$ whose arguments are of the same type as $\psi!\hat{z}$. ([PM], 74)

There are echoes of the construction of numbers as equivalence classes in this account of the no-class theory. Just as numbers are what classes have in common, classes might be thought of as what equivalent propositional functions have in common, namely, their extension. But what the things have "in common" is different in the two cases. For equinumerous classes it is membership in the equivalence class. The object that the classes have in common is another object, the equivalence class. What propositional functions have in common is an abstracted property, but still a property. What is common to "being a creature with a heart" and "being a creature with a kidney", is a function which picks out those same animals. Talk about (i.e., functions of) "the class" are to be represented as functions of those coextensive functions. What is needed is an account of the properties of this property that coextensive propositional functions have in common which will represent properties of the class. We can't just treat any function of functions as also a function of a class, for some will be intensional. Instead, as Russell says, he must *construct* an extensional function of functions which can be so interpreted. So the construction is twofold; we replace properties of classes with certain *constructed* functions of functions. The function f is true of the class $\hat{z}(\psi z)$ just in case $\psi\hat{z}$ has the constructed property of being equivalent to some predicative function $\phi!\hat{z}$ that satisfies f.[15] The no-class theory shares its logical form with the theory of descriptions, but its spirit with that of definition by abstraction.

Russell said that the theory of descriptions was the key to his solution of the paradoxes.[16] The no-class theory, with its contextual analysis of talk about classes, is indeed essential to the solution. As with other uses of constructions, however, it is not the denial of the constructed entity's existence that plays a role in Russell's analysis, but rather the logical import of the proposed analysis that really does the work. So it is not denying the existence of classes that resolves the paradoxes but rather the typed nature of propositional functions. Russell does speak of classes as not "... part of the ultimate constituents of your world" ([PLA], 234), and also claims that he is neutral as to their existence "as one" ([PM], 24). This should be taken to mean that classes are not individuals but rather their properties are those of entities higher up in the hierarchy of types. Russell says often that the lesson of the paradoxes was that classes are not objects, rather than simply that some predicates do not correspond with classes. One reason he gives is that there cannot be a totality of classes, "since there are more classes than individuals" ([IMP], 83).[17] That is the lesson of the paradox that was built on Cantor's original "diagonal" argument showing that for each cardinal number there is a larger.

Classes are seemingly all lowest level objects, so the hierarchy of properties, properties of properties, etc, does not solve the paradox by itself. The distinction between objects, classes, classes of classes, and so on, is not the same as the hierarchy of objects, properties, properties of properties, etc. The ramified theory of types takes a single level and splits it up. But these levels are all above the level of an individual. It does not split individuals into types.

Let us examine how the theory of types blocks Russell's paradox. Consider the analysis of a statement that a class is a member of itself:

---

[15]Böer [1973] points out that if f is a genuinely intensional function, say something about what someone believes, then it is unlikely that the derived expression will be equivalent to the original. After all, people may have beliefs about classes, but not about predicative functions, having never heard of the latter. The construction, however, does not attempt to reconstruct ordinary beliefs or to be an analysis of what those who talk about classes really mean. Rather, because of the paradoxes, we clearly must revise our attitudes toward classes. The construction of classes is clearly more of a *replacement* than an *analysis*.

[16]For example, at MPD (79).

[17]This theme can be found in the earliest discussions of the paradox, and even in its predecessor, what Moore calls the "Paradox of the Largest Cardinal" ([CP3], xxxii).

$\hat{z}(\psi z) \in \hat{z}(\psi z)$

The no-class theory ($*20\cdot01$), put into contemporary notation, states that:

$$f[\hat{z}(\psi z)] =_{df} (\exists \phi)[(\forall x)(\phi! x \equiv \psi x) \wedge f(\phi! \hat{z})]$$

Combined with ($*20\cdot02$), namely:

$$y \in \hat{z}(\phi! z) =_{df} \phi! y$$

the original statement yields:

$$\hat{z}(\psi z) \in \hat{z}(\psi z) \equiv \psi[\hat{z}(\psi z)]$$

which is equivalent to:

$$(\exists \phi)(\forall x)[(\phi! x \equiv \psi x) \wedge \psi(\phi! \hat{z})]$$

This last expression, however, violates the simple theory of types because $\psi!$ and $\phi!$ will be of the same type.

With an assumption of extensionality for propositional functions:

$$(\forall \phi)(\forall \psi)[f(\phi \hat{z}) \wedge (\forall x)(\phi x \equiv \psi x) \supset f(\psi \hat{z})]$$

we get the more blatant violation:

$$\hat{z}(\phi z) \in \hat{z}(\phi z) \equiv \phi(\phi \hat{z})$$

This formula quite obviously violates the vicious circle principle, by requiring a function to apply to itself. That classes are extensional is not needed to resolve the paradox, however, nor is the ramification of the theory of types, just as Ramsey said.

This way of presenting the paradoxes makes sense of Russell's view that the no-class theory is key to their solution. Seeing that classes are not objects is enough to resolve the paradox of sets. But this is not to say that classes simply do not exist. To see that they aren't objects is rather to see that they really play the same role as higher order entities, propositional functions, to which type distinctions do apply. They are not identified with functions, but everything said "about" them is something that is true of a function. It is propositional functions which have the logical features necessary for resolving the paradox. Replacing properties of classes (seen as objects) with properties of propositional functions allows logic to resolve the contradictions. In this sense when Ramsey says that the simple theory is enough to resolve the paradox, he is right. A certain aspect of the system of types of propositional functions provides the solution, not a classification of classes as objects into different levels. The extensionality of classes does not enter into the solution. That functions cannot apply to other functions of the same type is all that is needed, and nothing about the extensional nature of classes is involved. This solution of the paradoxes is thus at home in an intensional theory of propositional functions and is very different from the solution in axiomatic set theory which treats sets as objects in an extensional system.

7.4   CONSTRUCTING THE NUMBERS

In this section I will provide a brief examination of the way that Russell and Whitehead carry out the reduction of numbers to logic, to reveal the ontological aspects of that reduction. It is illuminating to compare this reduction with Frege's.[18] Frege was concerned solely with the derivation of the Peano-Dedekind axioms for numbers, first defining the primitive notions of 0, successor (rather, immediate predecessor) and Natural Number, then deriving the five axioms: (i) 0 is a number, (ii) every number is the immediate predecessor of a number, (iii) no number is the immediate predecessor of 0, (iv) the relation of immediate predecessor is functional, indeed the function is 1–1, and (v) the induction axiom, if 0 has a property and if given that a number x has a property and x is the immediate predecessor of y then y has the property, it follows that all numbers have the property. Richard Heck [1993] shows how in the derivation of these axioms, and also in the definitions of the primitive notions, no appeal is made to the properties of extensions (courses of values) of concepts beyond that needed to establish "Hume's Principle" as a lemma. Hume's principle is the thesis that the number of Fs = the number of Gs if and only if there is a one to one correspondence between Fs and Gs. Very little appeal is made to facts about extensions in any of rest of the derivations. The definitions of primitive notions do mention classes, but they have a definite logical flavor in comparison with Russell's. 0, for example, is defined as the number of the concept $[x \neq x]$. The definition of predecessor is also logical; m immediately preceeds n if and only if there is some concept F, n is the number of F and there is some x which is F such that m is the number of the concept $[Fz \wedge z \neq x]$. A careful examination of Frege's proofs, Heck concludes, shows that he avoided extensions as much as possible, and once used to define the notion of the number of a concept, in order to prove Hume's principle, they do not enter essentially into the subsequent proofs. Frege's project really is one of a reduction of mathematics to logic. Mathematics is first to be fully arithmetized, reduced to numbers and classes, showing that what is distinctive to mathematics is the theory of the numbers, and then that theory is to be reduced to genuinely logical notions, including, it seems somewhat reluctantly, the extensions of concepts when needed.

---

[18]I will follow the technical presentation of Heck [1993] who follows Frege's *Grundgesetze* rather than *Grundlagen*.

The reduction of mathematics to logic in PM is altogether different in tone. If anything it follows the reduction of mathematics to set theory following the work of Zermelo and Cantor which preceeded it. The theory of functions and relations (in extension) is developed in PM before numbers ever appear. When numbers are defined, it is not the natural numbers, but cardinals in general. The cardinal number of a set α, $Nc'\alpha$, is defined as the range of the equinumerosity relation sm, namely: $\hat{\beta}(\beta \, sm \, \alpha)$. 0 is defined as the unit set of the empty set, in modern notation $\{\phi\}$, but in PM notation[19]:

$$*54{\cdot}01 \quad 0 = \iota'\Lambda \quad Df$$

1 is the class of unit classes:

$$*52{\cdot}01 \quad 1 = \hat{\alpha}\{(\exists x).\alpha = \iota'x\} \quad Df$$

2 is the class of pairs:

$$*54{\cdot}02 \quad 2 = \hat{\alpha}\{(\exists x,y).x \neq y.\alpha = \iota'x \cup \iota'y\} \quad Df$$

The sum of two cardinal numbers is defined at $*110{\cdot}02$ as the cardinal of the sum of two classes α and β having those two cardinals. The sum of two sets is defined with this awkward notation:

$$*110{\cdot}01 \quad \alpha + \beta = \downarrow (\Lambda \cap \beta)\text{``}\iota\text{``}\alpha \cup (\Lambda \cap \alpha) \downarrow \text{``}\iota\text{``}\beta \quad Df$$

In more modern notation this is just the union of two sets equinumerous with α and β but guaranteed to be disjoint:

$$\{< \{x\}, \phi >: x \in \alpha\} \cup \{< \phi, \{y\} >: y \in \beta\}$$

These examples show that no attempt is made to reduce the mathematical or set theoretical content of the definitions as Frege did. What Russell and Whitehead present in PM is a fairly straightforward development of relations, functions and numbers in the style of Zermelo's axiomatic set theory. Underneath the exotic symbolism, modern readers will even find two standard proofs of the Schröder-Bernstein theorem and numerous other results familiar from what is now studied as "Axiomatic Set Theory".

Allen Hazen ([1984], 367) is puzzled by this similarity with axiomatic set theory when he considers the effects of adopting the axiom of reducibility. Russell suggests in ML and again at PM (166) that the axiom of reducibility, while an existence claim, is somehow weaker or less objectionable than postulating classes. Hazen asks how it is conceivable that Russell could have worked through a three volume development of

---

[19] The unit set containing x is formed with an operator '$\iota'x$'. The description symbol, '$\imath$', is intended to represent the converse operation, picking out the unique element of a singleton, the unique thing having a certain property.

set theory and mathematics without realizing that the system in which he was working could have the iterative conception of sets (or rather, the simple theory of types) embedded in it? He surely could not. The very development of numbers and mathematics that is given is in terms of classes that follow the iterative or Zermelo conception exactly. Russell clearly did see the universe of sets embedded, as predicative propositional functions, in his theory of types. To mathematicians and mathematically inclined logicians such as Quine and Gödel, the commitment to propositional functions seemed simply excessive. Why believe in objects that go beyond the cumulative hierarchy of sets in simple type theory? How could the result be seen as a reduction of mathematics to logic if the logic contained all the structure of the universe of sets and more?

The answer is that Russell's project was not one of ontological reduction, or ontological parsimony. The attempt was not to reduce the large ontology of mathematical objects to a smaller ontology of purely logical objects. Rather it was to *embed* mathematics in logic, to be able to derive the results of mathematics as special results in a more encompassing logical theory. The universe of propositional functions has all the structure of the universe of sets and more. Classes *as individuals* do not exist. Treating classes as individuals would require an improper collapse of what should be seen as a whole hierarchy of equivalent propositional functions. Rather than providing an ontological reduction of classes to propositional functions, the no-class theory provides a replacement of talk of classes by theses about some of the universe of propositional functions. The technique used is contextual definition, rather than of explicit definition, but the effect is not any more of a wholesale ontological elimination than is the theory of definite descriptions.

7.5   CONSTRUCTING MATTER

The construction of matter is our last example of a construction. This is a late development in Russell's philosophy.[20] Russell abandoned his earlier account of matter as the inferred cause of sense data, replacing it with an account of matter as constructed from those sense data directly. This shift might seem to be an application of Ockham's razor to eliminate inferred entities in favor of a construction of those already given in experience. One of Stebbing's criticisms was that Russell had confounded the case of the construction of classes or real numbers, where we substitute a precise notion for an obscure notion, with the case of tables and the like, where we want an analysis that is epistemologically correct. Before the construction was given, the notion of class or real

---

[20]See Miah [1987] for the origins and history of Russell's construction of matter.

number was obscure and seemingly subject to paradox. However, tables surely exist and we can know about them only in a certain fashion. What is in doubt is the correct logical analysis of sentences about tables and our evidence for such sentences. Russell is wrong to assimilate the regimentation of class talk to the analysis of table talk, Stebbing charged.

As I have presented it, however, Russell's project is not that of analysis of talk about matter. Russell's thesis was not phenomenalism as that is currently understood. Russell does not propose that talk about tables really is talk about sense data, as it would be were he proposing an analysis. Rather, he says, he wants to substitute something quite certain for talk about inferred entities that can never be known with any certainty.

> Matter, traditionally, has two of those 'neat' properties which are the mark of a logical construction; first, that two pieces of matter cannot be at the same place at the same time; secondly, that one piece of matter cannot be at two places at the same time. Experience in the substitution of constructions for inferences makes one suspicious of anything so tidy and exact. One cannot help feeling that impenetrability is not an empirical fact, derived from observation of billiard balls, but is something logically necessary. ([LA], 164)

What do we know for sure, given Russell's construction? Most importantly, we know that matter exists, in particular that some given object that is perceived exists. Second, we know that no two things could be in the same place at the same time, and other neat features of matter. What about claims about the real as opposed to observed properties of a thing, the real shape, color, etc.? These problems no longer exist, as there are only the observed qualities to account for and no primary qualities attributed to an inferred matter. This is different from the case of classes where the properties of classes (in particular the impossibility of self-membership) are shown to arise from the features of the functions from which they are constructed. That is more like a modern reduction. The geometric properties of matter are not shown to arise from the properties of sense data, but rather from the way in which matter is constructed from those sense data. It is the logical nature of those definitions that guarantees the logical status of the truths about matter. This is a replacement, or change of topic, rather than a reduction.

Russell has an unusual epistemological project. It seems as if he had taken precisely those questions for which there remained a Cartesian doubt, and showed how a construction could eliminate them. If, as he had earlier proposed, one were to infer the existence of matter as the cause of sense data, then there would be forever a possiblity of error, that there is in fact no cause outside of matter. As well, certain facts about matter, the neat ones, would be forever subject to sceptical doubts, their status misunderstood. Russell says that he has resolved doubt with his constructions by making a substitution:

> Things of that sort [atoms, particles, etc.], I say, are not the ultimate constituents of matter in any metaphysical sense. Those things are all of them, as I think a very little reflection shows, logical fictions in the sense that I was speaking of. At least, when I say they are, I speak somewhat too dogmatically. It is possible that there may be all these things that the physicist talks about in actual reality, but it is impossible that we should ever have any reason whatsoever for supposing that there are. That is the situation that you arrive at generally in such analyses. You find that a certain thing which has been set up as a metaphysical entity can either be assumed dogmatically to be real, and then you will have no possible argument either for its reality or against its reality; or, instead of doing that, you can construct a logical fiction having the same formal properties, or rather having formally analogous formal properties to those of the supposed metaphysical entity and itself composed of empirically given things, and that logical fiction can be substituted for your supposed metaphysical entity and will fulfill all the scientific purposes that anybody can desire. ([PLA], 236)

> I want to make it clear that I am not *denying* the existence of anything; I am only refusing to affirm it. I refuse to affirm the existence of anything for which there is no evidence, but I equally refuse to deny the existence of anything against which there is no evidence. ([PLA], 237)

This is not a case of finding evidence which is stronger to replace current, weaker inductive evidence about the existence of matter. Russell says that there is "no evidence" for these things that the physicist talks about. This is also clearly not the project of regimenting the talk of physicists such that their current vague and uncertain judgments can be replaced by some other more precise claims. What other project is served? It is "... all the scientific purposes that anybody could desire". That is not analysis or regimentation, but an actual replacement, a change of topic that allows certain scientific purposes to be preserved. The "purposes" are to meet the sceptical challenge to the very existence of matter, and to allow the proof, as logical properties, of the neat properties of matter. Regaining Cartesian certainty is not the only possible goal of such a project. Russell was impressed with the way that the theory of relativity might alter our conception of space, time and physical objects. It is quite possible that scientific theories might differ in their purposes and thus demand different constructions. Although I have stressed the serious ontological goals of much of Russell's use of constructions, there is nothing in the project of construction that commits it to claims about the unique ontology of the world.[21]

Viewing constructions as a replacement rather than analysis of ordinary talk puts Russell's project more in line with Carnap's later "logical construction of the world", with its equally problematic relation to more familiar projects of other philosophers.[22] It is the novelty of Russell's project that makes Stebbing compare it with more familiar ones and conclude that it is somehow a confusion of several of them. It is in fact none of them, but another altogether.

7.6   CONSTRUCTIONS AND FORMAL SEMANTICS

What then is the picture of logical constructions that emerges from my account? Logical constructions are modelled on Frege's definition by abstraction of numbers. That was a definition by abstraction designed to make derivable what had previously been taken as postulates. While Russell's construction might avoid postulating problematic entities such as classes in favor of more familiar individuals and propositional functions, its primary purpose was not ontological reduction, and in particular not nominalist reduction, as the term 'logical fiction' might suggest. Russell was prepared to quantify over entities that were to be constructed, and even, in the case of propositional functions, to attribute to them an ontological dependence determined by their construction. When, under the influence of Whitehead, Russell turned the technique of construction to matter, he kept its distinctive features, including the most startling of all, the shift of subject matter away from the ordinary conception of matter to another, whereby the neat properties of matter could be directly proved.

What became of this project of logical construction? It has persisted in several different areas. One is the project of finding *set theoretic* constructions. Consider the case of propositions. Now it is natural to think of singular or Russellian propositions as ordered *sequences* where those

---

[21] R.E. Tully points out that in the above passage from Russell ([LA], 164) there is a tone of irony, suggesting that Russell is suspicious of "neat" properties. I take these passages to suggest that he might consider them to be theory relative.

[22] Notwithstanding Michael Friedman's [1992] attempts to align that project with the neo-Kantian notion of *constitution* of the world.

in turn are seen as sets of a certain sort. When pressed, one may acknowledge that propositions are not really sets, but they can be *modelled* by them. Construction is essential to the related project of finding a set theoretic *model* for a given formal theory. One can see using sets or ordered pairs, say, as the interpretation of two place relation symbols, as a case of construction at work. A set theoretic object has been found that can serve the model theoretic purposes of relations. Indeed, in some sense, any model of a group of sentences can be seen as containing a *construction* of the objects those sentences are taken to be about. No one would see a model as an analysis of a notion, except in the sense of providing "semantics" for talk about the notion. That seems to be what happened to the the project of logical construction. It became the project of providing set theoretic constructions that could enter into the formal semantics of a formalized theory. This semantic project is also neither a regimentation nor an analysis of ordinary talk, nor does it have an obvious relevance to epistemological concerns.[23] The test of constructions now is not whether they allow proofs of the right neat facts about the objects themselves, but rather of conditionals (in fact biconditionals) stating conditions on constructed objects materially equivalent to conditions on ordinary objects. So, rather than directly constructing properties as sets of objects and proving neat facts about properties by proxy, we assert biconditionals, such as that an object has a property if and only if it is in a certain set. The set theoretic constructions of formal semantics are the direct descendents of Russell's logical constructions. Thus Russell's notion of logical construction can be seen to survive still, though not as a central part of the project of analytic philosophy. Its decline, however, is more due to its remarkable success. We know that any given structural features of objects can be modelled with sets. Fitting those constructions together, however, so as to provide the truth conditions of a body of sentences in a systematic way is not easy. The project of construction has become the project of providing formal semantics. It is a characteristically Russellian notion that often what starts out in philosophy as a controversial and obscure notion may be made precise through analysis and end up as a routine scientific tool.

Indeed this was the result of Russell's whole logical project after this period. With the rise of extensional first order logic in combination with the axiomatic treatment of sets, any sort of construction or higher type entity was to be developed as a construction in set theory. Logicians followed Ramsey's analysis of the paradoxes into those solved by set theory

---

[23]This is particularly seen in "actualist" attempts to "construct" possible worlds from existing entities such as propositions. David Lewis [1986] calls these "ersatz" worlds.

and those due to semantics. With Tarski's formal account of semantics, the later paradoxes also entered the domain of set theory. Intensional paradoxes were simply ignored in the move to extensional logic. The rise of interest in syntax among logicians, combined with the extensionalism, led also to a rise of nominalism with regard to universals. The distinctive realist features of Russell's ontology were thus also abandoned. The views of Quine, who can be seen as Russell's main proponent and follower in North America, illustrate this progress. Quine has defended extensionalism, nominalism and the use of set theory as a basis for constructions of notions to replace those that give philosophical problems.[24] A look back at Russell's earlier project might help those wondering where to go from here.

---

[24]See, for example, his analysis of the semantic paradoxes as a result in set theory, a proof that a particular set, which would be defined by the relational predicate "satisfies", does not exist. See Quine ([1986], 44–46) for this point, and elsewhere for the rest of these views on logic.

8

POSTSCRIPT ON LOGICISM

The preceding discussions are intended to reveal the metaphysical underpinnings of Russell's logic. The nature and status of propositional functions and propositions, the theory of types, the axiom of reducibility, as well as Russell's various logical constructions, all depend on his views about ontology and dependence. This view of logic differs sharply from the view that succeeded Russell beginning in the 1920s.[1] Logic came to be seen as a formal system in which partially interpreted symbolic languages are used to represent sentences. Focus shifted from the truth of logical principles to their *validity*, which in turn came to be seen, in a model theoretic sense, as true on all "interpretations". From this new point of view Russell's logicist project of reducing mathematics to logic was seen as unsuccessful. Two lines of criticism converged on the conclusion that Russell's brand of logicism in PM was a failure. One was criticism of the seemingly non-logical assumptions of that work, namely, the axiom of reducibility, the "multiplicative" axiom and the axiom of infinity. Gödel, for one, charges that these are not analytic truths but rather existence claims, claims of the same sort as those in axiomatic set theory.[2] Indeed two of these axioms, the multiplicative axiom and the axiom of infinity, show up explicitly in Zermelo Frankel set theory as axioms, the former as the axiom of "choice". Russell did have qualms about including such existence claims in logic, and in PM considers the axiom of infinity to be a tacit hypothesis of theorems which require it. Gödel's criticism is that a theory postulating basic mathematical enti-

---

[1] See, for example, Goldfarb [1979].

[2] At Gödel ([1944], 150–151). The view that these are not logical principles (or analytic) is widely shared. See, for example, Carnap [1931], who tries to save the logicist program despite these failings of Russell's version. Boolos [1994], acknowledging Carnap's destinction between definitions in logic and derivations in logic, claims that Russell had quietly abandoned logicism by the time of PM. Boolos suggests that Russell had settled for just being able to express all mathematical notions using notions of logic rather than the full logicist project of then deriving all mathematical principles, so expressed, from logical principles alone.

ties, such as set theory, or the axioms asserting the existence of certain propositional functions, are perhaps a foundational theory for mathematics, but not to be counted as logic. This view has been crystalized in the opinion that while the rest of mathematics may be reduced to set theory, as the logicists showed, the reduction of set theory to logic was a failure.

The second line of criticism of logicism also derives from Gödel, this one from his famous first incompleteness theorem, found in "On Formally Undecidable Propositions of *Principia Mathematica* and Related Systems I" [1931]. That result shows that any formal system capable of representing the sentences of arithmetic and deriving Peano's axioms must be incomplete. Some truths of arithmetic will be unprovable for any such system. Gödel makes it clear that what he means by a formal system is what we would now call a system with a recursively enumerable set of axioms and decidable inference rules.[3] It is the syntactic nature of formal systems and the algorithmic nature of derivation in those systems that is essential for the proof. The lesson has been learned and absorbed in the doctrine that higher order logic (and hence the logic of PM) is not recursively enumerable, and hence not completely formalizable. Rather than quibble over what deserves the title of "logic" the argument should turn to whether Russell's reduction accomplishes the original goals of logicism. Logical truths must be analytic, it is thought, hence it should be possible merely by understanding the meanings of the expressions of logical truths to see that they are truths. The possibility of such knowledge requires that the truths of logic be effectively enumerable, and if that is so, Gödel has shown that mathematics cannot be reduced to logic.

Russell describes his logicist project in the opening sections of *Principles of Mathematics*, which begins with the claim:

> Pure Mathematics is the class of all propositions of the form "*p* implies *q*," where *p* and *q* are propositions containing one or more variables, the same in the two propositions, and neither *p* nor *q* contains any constants except logical constants. ([PoM], 3)

He identifies this project with Leibniz's, characterized by "The general doctrine that all mathematics is deduction by logical principles from logical principles ... ". The logical concepts are specified by enumeration from a small list, and extend to those definable in terms of those primitive concepts. The epistemological content of the project is summarized thus:

---

[3]He makes this clear in a note added to the paper in 1963. He takes Turing's analysis of formal system to be conclusive.

The connection of mathematics with logic, according to the
above account, is exceedingly close. The fact that all mathematical constants are logical constants, and that all the pre-
misses of mathematics are concerned with these, gives, I believe, the precise statement of what philosophers have meant
in asserting that mathematics is *à priori*. ([PoM], 8)

Both analyticity and formalism are missing from this characterization
of logic and logicism. Indeed in *Principles of Mathematics* ([PoM], 456)
Russell explicitly says that Kant was wrong, and that "... logic is just
as synthetic as all other kinds of truth ...". For Russell, analytic truths
are those derivable from logical laws and definitions. Primitive logical
laws then cannot be so derived, and thus are synthetic. Russell's view of
a priori truth, especially later in PoP (chapter X), is far removed from
analytic truth or anything which would be effectively decidable. In PoP
a priori truth results from the relations of universals, to be detected only
following acquaintance with those universals. It is true that *understanding* a proposition will show that it is a priori, but for that we must be
acquainted with universals and particulars named in it.[4] For logic to
be a priori, then, it does not have to be syntactically or in some other
way effectively formalized. Even the deductive nature of logic does not
require such effective formalization. Russell acknowledges a distinction
between "primitive propositions" of logic from which the others are to
be derived, and finds it valuable to minimize the number of primitive
propositions. However, the choice of primitive propositions is to some
extent a pragmatic matter, for it is the fruitfulness in deriving acknowledged principles of logic that determines what to take as primitive. It is
the generality and independence of empirical facts which makes principles *a priori* and logical, not some simplicity or syntactic feature which
is automatically or mechanically detectable.

The metaphysical aspects of Russell's logic described above fit with
this synthetic view of logicism. Primitive predicates of the language correspond with universals. Which propositional functions there are will
thus not be deducible on some syntactic grounds alone. Principles such
as the axiom of reducibility are not logically valid, but instead express a
view about the metaphysical analysis of propositional functions. The
multiplicative axiom does seem to be originally a description of the
structure of classes, but becomes a discovery about the structure of

---

[4]Coffa ([1991], chapter 7) contains an extended discussion of these issues. The
only notion of analytic or a priori truth that would be congenial to Russell would be
one on which the analysis of a proposition revealed its truth. That analysis is not a
study of language, but rather of the objects that are the meanings of words. Such a
procedure need not be effective or decidable at all.

the universe of functions. The construction of classes from propositional functions leads to the discovery of propositional functions and relations between them that are like those of sets seen as primitive objects. In sum then, the distinction between logic and metaphysics or ontology is blurred on this account. It is precisely these metaphysical aspects of Russell's logic that were felt to be incompatible with the success of logicism. Logicism then succeeds, but only with an extended or revised conception of logic.

Russell was not completely indifferent to the views behind these criticisms. As was seen above, he did have qualms about the "mathematical" axioms of reducibility, infinity and choice. His qualms, however, were directed at their not having the fully general nature necessary to logical truths. As such the distinction between logic and mathematics is one of generality, a matter of degree rather than of kind. As for formalization, this was to accomplish the goals of finding out all the hidden assumptions in mathematical proofs and of making definitions explicit.[5] Russell does not see logic as inherently formal in the syntactic sense necessary for Gödel's results. My study of the metaphysical nature of Russell's logic, then, may help to appreciate the status of Russell's logicist project, even to suggest that it was successful on its own terms.

---

[5]See his remarks about symbolism at PM (2–3).

REFERENCES

Anderson, C. Anthony. 1989. "Russellian Intensional Logic", in *Themes from Kaplan*, Joseph Almog, John Perry, and Howard Wettstein, eds. Oxford: Oxford University Press, 67–103.

Aristotle. 1984. *Categories*, in *The Complete Works of Aristotle*, Jonathan Barnes, ed. Princeton: Princeton University Press, 3–24.

Armstrong, David M. 1978. *Nominalism and Realism: Universals and Scientific Realism*, Vol. I. Cambridge: Cambridge University Press.

———. 1997. *A World of States of Affairs*. Cambridge: Cambridge University Press.

Barwise, Jon and John Etchemendy. 1987. *The Liar*. Oxford: Oxford University Press.

Böer, Steven E. 1973. "Russell on Classes as Logical Fictions", *Analysis* 33, 206–208.

Boolos, George. 1994. "The Advantages of Honest Toil over Theft", in *Mathematics and Mind*, Alexander George, ed. Oxford: Oxford University Press, 27–44.

Carnap, Rudolf. 1931. "Symposium on the Foundations of Mathematics: The Logicist Foundations of Mathematics", in *Philosophy of Mathematics: Selected Readings*, 2nd ed., Paul Benacceraf and Hilary Putnam, eds. Cambridge: Cambridge University Press, 1983, 41–52.

Chihara, Charles. 1973. *Ontology and the Vicious Circle Principle*. Ithaca, NY: Cornell University Press.

Church, Alonzo. 1956. *Introduction to Mathematical Logic*, Vol. I. Princeton, NJ: Princeton University Press.

143

————. 1974. "Russellian Simple Type Theory", in *Proceedings and Addresses of the American Philosophical Association* 47, 747–760.

————. 1976. "Comparison of Russell's Resolution of the Semantical Antinomies with That of Tarski", *Journal of Symbolic Logic* 41, 747–760.

————. 1984. "Russell's Theory of the Identity of Propositions", *Philosophia Naturalis* 21, 513–522.

Chwistek, Leon. 1921. "Antinomies of Formal Logic", in *Polish Logic: 1920–1939*, Storrs McCall, ed. Oxford: Clarendon Press, 1967, 338–345.

Cocchiarella, Nino. 1980. "The Development of the Theory of Logical Types and the Notion of a Logical Subject in Russell's Early Philosophy", *Synthese* 45, 71–115.

————. 1991. "Bertrand Russell" in *Handbook of Metaphysics and Ontology*, Vol. II, H. Burkhardt and B. Smith, eds. Munich: Philosophia, 796–798.

Coffa, J. Alberto. 1991. *The Semantic Tradition from Kant to Carnap: To the Vienna Station*. Cambridge: Cambridge University Press.

Copi, Irving. 1971. *The Theory of Logical Types*. London: Routledge and Kegan Paul.

Dummett, Michael. 1981. *Frege: Philosophy of Language*, 2nd ed. London: Duckworth.

Evans, Gareth. 1982. *The Varieties of Reference*. Oxford: Oxford University Press.

Frege, Gottlob. 1884. *The Foundations of Arithmetic*, J.L. Austin, trans. Evanston, Ill.: Northwestern University Press, 1980.

————. 1892. "On Sense and Meaning", in *Collected Papers on Mathematics, Logic and Philosophy*, B. McGuiness, ed. Oxford: Basil Blackwell, 1984, 157–177.

————. 1980. *Philosophical and Mathematical Correspondence*, G. Gabriel et. al., eds. Chicago: University of Chicago Press.

Friedman, Michael. 1992. "Epistemology in the *Aufbau*", *Synthese* 93, 15–74.

Geach, Peter T. 1956. *Mental Acts*. London: Routledge and Kegan Paul.

Gödel, Kurt. 1931. "On Formally Undecidable Propositions of *Principia*

Mathematica and Related Systems I", in *From Frege to Gödel: A Source Book in Mathematical Logic, 1879–1931*, Jean van Heijenoort, ed. Cambridge Mass: Harvard University Press, 1967, 596–616.

———. 1944. "Russell's Mathematical Logic", in *The Philosophy of Bertrand Russell*, P.A. Schilpp, ed. LaSalle, Ill.: Open Court, 125–153.

Goldfarb, Warren. 1979. "Logic in the Twenties: The Nature of the Quantifier", *Journal of Symbolic Logic* 44, 351–368.

———. 1989. "Russell's Reasons for Ramification", in *Rereading Russell: Essays on Bertrand Russell's Metaphysics and Epistemology*, C.W. Savage and C.A. Anderson, eds. Minnesota Studies in the Philosophy of Science, Vol. XII. Minneapolis: University of Minnesota Press, 24–40.

Griffin, Nicholas. 1980. "Russell on the Nature of Logic (1903–1913)', *Synthese* 45, 117–188.

———. 1985. "Russell's Multiple Relation Theory of Judgment', *Philosophical Studies* 47, March, 213–248.

Hager, Paul J. 1994. *Continuity and Change in the Development of Russell's Philosophy*. Dordrecht and Boston: Kluwer Academic Publishers.

Hatcher, William S. 1968. *Foundations of Mathematics*. Philadelphia: W.B. Saunders.

Hazen, Allen. 1983. "Predicative Logics", chapter I.5 in *Handbook of Philosophical Logic*, Vol. I, D. Gabbay and F. Guenthner, eds. Dordrecht: D. Reidel, 331–407.

Heck, Richard G. 1993. "The Development of Arithmetic in Frege's *Grundgesetze der Arithmetik*", *The Journal of Symbolic Logic*, 58, 579–601.

Hylton, Peter. 1980. "Russell's Substitutional Theory", *Synthese* 45, 1–31.

———. 1989. "The Significance of 'On Denoting' ", in *Rereading Russell: Essays on Bertrand Russell's Metaphysics and Epistemology*, C. Wade Savage and C. Anthony Anderson, eds. Minnesota Studies in the Philosophy of Science, Vol. XII. Minneapolis: University of Minnesota Press, 88–107.

————. 1990. *Russell, Idealism, and the Emergence of Analytic Philosophy.* Oxford: Oxford University Press.

Johnson, W.E. 1964. *Logic: Part I.* New York: Dover.

Jung, Darryl. 1994. "The Logic of *Principia Mathematica*", Ph.D. Dissertation, Department of Linguistics and Philosophy, Massachusetts Institute of Technology.

Kaplan, David. 1972. "What is Russell's Theory of Descriptions?", in *Bertrand Russell, A Collection of Critical Essays*, D.F. Pears, ed. New York: Doubleday Anchor, 227–244.

————. 1989, "Demonstratives", in *Themes from Kaplan*, Joseph Almog, John Perry, and Howard Wettstein, eds. Oxford: Oxford University Press, 481–563.

Kazmi, Ali. 1990. "Parthood and Persistence", in *Canadian Philosophers, Canadian Journal of Philosophy, Supplementary Volume 16*, David Copp, ed. Calgary: University of Calgary Press, 227–250.

Landini, Gregory. 1987. "Russell's Substitutional Theory of Classes and Relations", *History and Philosophy of Logic*, 8, 171–200.

————. 1993. "Reconciling PM's Ramified Type Theory with the Doctrine of the Unrestricted Variable of the *Principles*", in *Russell and Analytic Philosophy*, A.D. Irvine and G.A. Wedeking, eds. Toronto: University of Toronto Press, 361–394.

————. 1996. "Will the Real *Principia Mathematica* Please Stand Up? Reflections on the Formal Logic of the *Principia*", in *Bertrand Russell and the Origins of Analytic Philosophy*, R. Monk and A. Palmer, eds. Bristol: Toemmes.

————. 1998. *Russell's Hidden Substitutional Theory.* New York and Oxford: Oxford University Press.

Lewis, David. 1986. *On the Plurality of Worlds.* Oxford: Basil Blackwell.

Linsky, Bernard. 1988. "Propositional Functions and Universals in *Principia Mathematica*", *Australasian Journal of Philosophy* 66, Dec., 447–460.

————. 1990. "Was the Axiom of Reducibility a Principle of Logic?", *Russell, The Journal of the Bertrand Russell Archives* 10, Winter, 125–140.

————. 1993. "Why Russell Abandoned Russellian Propositions", in

Russell and Analytic Philosophy, A.D. Irvine and G.A. Wedeking, eds. Toronto: University of Toronto Press, 193–209.

———. 1995. "Russell's Logical Constructions", in *Studies in Dialectics of Nature* (Beijing), Vol. 11 Supplementary Issue, 129–148.

———. 1996. Review of: Gregory H. Moore, ed., *Toward the "Principles of Mathematics" 1900–02. The Collected Papers of Bertrand Russell, Vol.3*, in *Philosophia Mathematica* (3), 4, 1996, 73–78.

Linsky, Leonard. 1983. *Oblique Contexts*. Chicago: University of Chicago Press.

———. 1987. "Russell's 'No-Classes' Theory of Classes", in *On Being and Saying: Essays for Richard Cartwright*, J.J. Thomson, ed. Cambridge, Mass.: MIT Press, 21–39.

Miah, Sajahan. 1987. "The Emergence of Russell's Logical Construction of Physical Objects", in *Russell: The Journal of the Bertrand Russell Archives* 7, 11–24.

Monk, Ray. 1990. *Ludwig Wittgenstein: The Duty of Genius*. New York: Free Press.

———. 1996. "What is Analytical Philosophy?", in *Bertrand Russell and the Origins of Analytical Philosophy*. Bristol: Thoemmes, 1–22.

Myhill, John. 1974. "The Undefinability of the Set of Natural Numbers in the Ramified Principia", in *Bertrand Russell's Philosophy*, George Nakhnikian, ed. London: Duckworth, 19–27.

———. 1979. "A Refutation of an Unjustified Attack on the Axiom of Reducibility", in *Bertrand Russell Memorial Volume*, H.D. Lewis, ed. London: George Allen and Unwin, 81–90.

Neale, Stephen. 1990. *Descriptions*. Cambridge, Mass.: MIT Press.

Olson, Kenneth. 1987. *An Essay on Facts*. CSLI Lecture Notes No. 6. Stanford: CSLI Publications.

Pelham, Judith M. 1993. *Russell on Propositions and Objects*, Ph.D. Dissertation, Department of Philosophy, University of Toronto.

Perkins, R.K. 1972. "Urmson on Russell's Incomplete Symbols", *Analysis* 32.6, 200–203.

———. 1974. "Incomplete Symbols Again – A reply to Mr. Urmson", *Analysis* 35.1, 29–31.

Quine, Willard van Orman. 1966. "Russell's Ontological Development", *Journal of Philosophy* 63, 657–667.

––––––. 1961. "Logic and the Reification of Universals", in *From a Logical Point of View*. New York: Harper and Row, 1963.

––––––. 1963. *Set Theory and Its Logic*. Cambridge, Mass.: Harvard University Press.

––––––. 1986. *Philosophy of Logic*. Cambridge, Mass.: Harvard University Press.

Ramsey, Frank P. 1965. *The Foundations of Mathematics*. Littlefield, Adams & Co.

Richards, John. 1980. "Propositional Functions and Russell's Philosophy of Language, 1903–1914", *Philosophical Forum* XI(4), 315–339.

Russell, Bertrand. 1900. *The Philosophy of Leibniz*. 2nd ed., reprinted 1992. London: Routledge. [PL]

––––––. 1903. *Principles of Mathematics*. 2nd ed. 1928. New York: W.W. Norton. [PoM]

––––––. 1905. "On Denoting", reprinted in Robert Marsh, ed., *Logic and Knowledge: Essays 1901–1950*. London: George Allen and Unwin, 1956, 39–56. [OD]

––––––. 1906. "On 'Insolubilia' and Their Solution in Symbolic Logic", in *Essays in Analysis*, D. Lackey, ed. New York: George Braziller, 1973. [OI]

––––––. 1908. "Mathematical Logic as Based on the Theory of Types", in *Logic and Knowledge: Essays 1901–1950*, Robert Marsh, ed. London: George Allen and Unwin, 1956, 57–102. [ML]

––––––. 1910. "Knowledge by Acquaintance and Knowledge by Description", in *Mysticism and Logic*. London: Allen and Unwin, 1963. [KAD]

––––––. 1911. "On the Relations of Universals and Particulars", in *Logic and Knowledge*, R. Marsh, ed. London: George Allen and Unwin, 1956. [RUP]

––––––. 1912. *The Problems of Philosophy*. Reprinted 1967. Oxford: Oxford University Press. [PoP]

––––––. 1918. "The Philosophy of Logical Atomism", in CP8, 160–244. References to this edition. Also in *The Philosophy of Logical Atomism*, David Pears, ed. LaSalle, Ill.: Open Court, 1985. [PLA]

————. 1919. *Introduction to Mathematical Philosophy*, 1st ed. Reprinted 1993. London: Routledge. [IMP]

————. 1924. "Logical Atomism", reprinted in *The Philosophy of Logical Atomism*, D.F. Pears, ed. LaSalle, Ill: Open Court, 1985, 157–181. [LA]

————. 1931. "Review of Ramsey", *Foundations of Mathematics, Mind* 40, 476–82. [RR1]

————. 1932. "Review of Ramsey", *Foundations of Mathematics, Philosophy* 7, 84–86. [RR2]

————. 1959. *My Philosophical Development*. London: George Allen and Unwin. [MPD]

————. 1984. *Theory of Knowledge*, in *The Collected Papers of Bertrand Russell*, Vol. 7. London: George Allen and Unwin. [ToK]

————. 1986. *The Collected Papers of Bertrand Russell*, Vol. 8, *The Philosophy of Logical Atomism and Other Essays: 1914–1919*, John G. Slater, ed. London, Allen and Unwin. [CP8]

————. 1992. *The Collected Papers of Bertrand Russell*, Vol. 6, *Logical and Philosophical Papers: 1909–13*, John G. Slater, ed. London: Routledge. [CP6]

————. 1993. *The Collected Papers of Bertrand Russell*, Vol. 3, *Toward the "Principles of Mathematics" 1900–02*, G.H. Moore, ed. London: Routledge. [CP3]

Ryle, Gilbert, 1979. "Bertrand Russell: 1872–1970", *Bertrand Russell Memorial Volume*, G.W. Roberts, ed. London: George Allen and Unwin, 15–21.

Sainsbury, R.M. 1980. "Russell on Constructions and Fictions", *Theoria* 46, 19–36.

Schütte, Kurt. 1960. *Beweistheorie*. Berlin: Springer Verlag.

Stebbing, L. Susan. 1930. *A Modern Introduction to Logic*. London: Methuen.

Urmson, J.O. 1956. *Philosophical Analysis*. Oxford: Oxford University Press.

————. 1973. "Russell's Incomplete Symbols", *Analysis*, 33.3, 111–112.

Wang, Hao. 1974. *From Mathematics to Philosophy*. London: Routledge and Kegan Paul.

Whitehead, A.N. 1926. Letter to the Editor, *Mind* 35, 130.

———. 1929. *Process and Reality*. Cambridge: Cambridge University Press.

Whitehead, A.N. and Bertrand Russell. 1910–1913. *Principia Mathematica*. 2nd ed., 1925–1927. Cambridge: Cambridge University Press. [PM]

Wisdom, John. 1931. "Logical Constructions (I.).", *Mind* XL, 188–216.

Wittgenstein, Ludwig. 1922. *Tractatus Logico-Philosophicus*. London: Routledge and Kegan Paul.

———. 1953. *Philosophical Investigations*. London: Macmillan.